By Love Refined

Dearest Dad & Mum,

Please enjoy this, from one of
my favourite philosophers/ human
beings. Both she & her husband
Dietrich are famous Catholic
philosophers.   Love, Michael

Books from
Sophia Institute Press
by Dietrich von Hildebrand:

Confidence in God
Humility: Wellspring of Virtue
Marriage: The Mystery of Faithful Love
Making Christ's Peace a Part of Your Life
Trojan Horse in the City of God
Transformation in Christ

Alice von Hildebrand

By Love Refined

Letters to a Young Bride

SOPHIA INSTITUTE PRESS®
Manchester, New Hampshire

Sophia Institute Press®
Box 5284, Manchester, NH 03108
1-800-888-9344
www.sophiainstitute.com

Library of Congress Cataloging-in-Publication Data

Von Hildebrand, Alice, 1923-
   By love refined : letters to a young bride / by Alice von Hildebrand.
   ISBN 0-918477-06-9 (hdbk. : alk. paper)
   ISBN 0-918477-51-4 (pbk. : alk. paper)
   1. Marriage. 2. Interpersonal relations.   I. Title.
HQ734.V66 1989
306.8′1 — dc19   88-34640 CIP

02 03 04 05 10 9 8 7 6 5 4

For my friends
Maedel Hutton
and
Nick & Jane Healy
– with gratitude.

*Where heart-room is,
     there house-room is always to be found.*
Sören Kierkegaard

Contents

By Love Refined

"Love is a great thing!"

Dear Julie,

At last, your deep longing is fulfilled: to love a man, to be loved by him, and to be freely bound to him in marriage "until death do you part."

Now your great mission begins. Together, you and Michael must weave into the tapestry of your life the many themes we discussed during your engagement: the beauty of marriage – its tasks, its joys – and love's power to lighten its burdens and sorrows.

I know how deeply you've understood the words of Thomas à Kempis, "Love is a great thing." Marriage is also a great thing: the most complete, the most intense, and the most beautiful relationship possible between two human beings.

But like all great things in life, marriage is a risk – a "deed of daring" (as Kierkegaard said). That's why a happy marriage is impossible for people who never take any step that might threaten their security. You and Michael now have in your hands the power to create an earthly heaven or hell. It's no secret that marriage can quickly become a hell for spouses. But remember that humanly speaking, a great love between husband and wife can also be the deepest source of happiness this side of heaven.

How awe-inspiring to see the beauty of another soul, to love him, and then to be permitted to share in his intimacy, actually to become one with him! There's no earthly experience that is greater than this unity of souls, minds, hearts, and bodies in marriage, which is why my husband always called it a "remnant of earthly paradise."

Such sublime spousal love is a gift, but a gift that must be nurtured and sheltered. Because of human imperfections, difficulties crop up in marriage, even between people (like you and Michael) who love each other deeply. I think you'll soon find that for this reason, although love is a gift, it must also be learned, especially as you try to relate it to your daily life which isn't lived in a fairy tale castle but in the midst of everyday pressures, problems, and trials.

No outsider or institution can guarantee that you and Michael will achieve joy in your marriage. You'll have to face the problems of marriage yourselves. Your success won't depend on exterior circumstances, but on your own inner attitudes: are you both willing to fight the good fight for your marriage, trusting that your mutual love, strengthened by grace, will achieve victory in spite of the tempests that threaten every human undertaking?

I know that you've already begun to experience the hopes and delights of marriage, and that you'll continue to do so in the coming months. My heart is filled with joy for you!

Your devoted friend,

Lily

"Setting up house takes so much work!"

Dear Julie,

What a contrast between the enchantment of your wedding, the delight of your honeymoon, and the many chores you now face in setting up a household and running it smoothly on a limited budget. I'm glad to see that you've carried into these tasks the joy of being in love, which lightens every burden.

Although it will be more difficult now by letter instead of in person, I'll try to continue to share with you insights from my own marriage and from hundreds of my married friends and students who've confided in me over the years.

We've traveled this road already, and perhaps our experiences can help you and Michael avoid some of our mistakes, as you undertake your immediate task of setting up a home together.

Setting up house takes so much work!

This is especially difficult, since home must be so much more than just a place to eat and sleep. It should be that mysterious enclosure in which your two lives can take root, a place where you both are sheltered, protected, far away from the hustle and bustle of professional life. It should become the place where you can rest spiritually and can dare to be yourselves because you know you're loved.

Each of you now has a calling to create this spiritual "space" in which your two lives can blossom. This is very different from earning a salary, fixing the car, doing the laundry, or washing the dishes.

Your own mission as wife goes far beyond household chores which could be done just as well by hired help. You must create a nest of love, a place where it's good to be.

What a world of difference there is between doing menial tasks to make money and to pay bills, and doing them because you rejoice in creating a home for your beloved Michael, the person closest to you on earth!

Seen from the outside, the stained-glass windows in a church look dull and dark; but when you enter the church and can see the same windows illumined by the rays of the sun, you discover their incredible beauty.

The light of the sun can transform stained-glass windows into magnificent works of art. Likewise, you can let your love for Michael transform the small, boring tasks of everyday life into magnificent works of love.

With all my affection,

Lily

"Lovers can't be concerned with little things."

Dear Julie,

I'm grateful for your frankness. It makes my duties as your godmother easier to fulfill.

You say that although the analogy of the stained-glass windows is very moving, nonetheless true lovers are concerned with "great things, beautiful things" and should not let themselves be troubled by small things.

Roy wouldn't agree.

He and my friend Evelyn have been married thirty-five years. She's sloppy and he's meticulous. During their honeymoon, Roy noticed that she always left the toothpaste tube open. He asked Evelyn to put the cap on, but she laughed at him, claiming he had the habits of an old maid. Time and again, Roy has asked her to change. Nothing doing! After thirty-five years, the cap still remains off and Roy has resigned himself to it.

Compare this to my own husband's attitude. Early in our marriage, I noticed he would always leave the soap swimming in a small pool of water. It would slowly disintegrate into an unattractive, slimy goo – something I found unappealing. I drew it to his attention. From that day on, he made a point of drying the soap after each use – to such an extent that I couldn't tell from the "soap testimony" whether he had washed himself or not. (Moreover – and this is typical of him – he too developed a strong dislike for sticky soap.) I was so moved by this, that to this day I feel a wave of loving gratitude for this small but significant gesture of love.

My husband was a great lover. And because he was one, he managed to relate the smallest things to love and was willing to change to please his beloved in all legitimate things. This characteristic is typical of great love.

I'm sure that as your love grows deeper, you, too, will come to see how the greater the love, the more it permeates even the smallest aspects of life.

With love,

Lily

"Yes, he's the right man for me."

Dear Julie,

I'm glad to hear your love for Michael has deepened in the four weeks you've known him as husband (rather than as fiancé). It's clear that you've truly been granted "the eyes of love."

Usually, we encounter in others only a caricature of their being; we are only able to discern what they've made of themselves rather than what they're meant to be.

In other cases, we see only what others allow us to see, for they hide their true selves because they've been wounded so often or they're shy or they fear they'll be misunderstood.

Yet, even though we don't often see it, all people are created in God's image and likeness; each one in some mysterious way reflects Him and has within himself an incredible beauty, which is mostly covered by the dust and dirt of sin.

When you fell in love with Michael, you were given a great gift: your love took you past appearances and granted you a perception of his true self, who he's meant to be in the deepest sense of the word. You discovered his "secret name."

Those who love have been granted the special privilege of seeing with incredible intensity the beauty of the one they love – while others see primarily his exterior acts, and particularly his failings. At this moment, you see Michael more clearly than does any other living human being.

I can illustrate this best with a story from the Gospel (which is so illuminating that even an unbeliever can profit from it). Do you recall the Gospel story of the Transfiguration? The apostles went with Jesus to the top of Mount Tabor, and suddenly Jesus became radiant and his garments a dazzling white. For the first time, the apostles were allowed to see Jesus directly, clothed in His glory as God. He was transfigured before them.

Similarly, when you fell in love with Michael, you saw his true face, his unique beauty: with the eyes of love, you were granted a "Tabor vision" of Michael.

Trust this bright Tabor vision you've been given. Daily rekindle it in your heart and let it nurture your love. If you let it form the cornerstone of your faithfulness to Michael, your marriage will be rich, indeed.

With all my love,

Lily

"Why do they say 'love is blind'?"

Dear Julie,

Don't allow yourself to be upset by the remarks you overheard at the Fourth of July picnic. It's not surprising that your co-workers can't understand why you fell in love with Michael.

Keep in mind that the person who sees is qualified to pass judgment on the thing he sees; but he who doesn't see is by his own admission blind. You perceive Michael's goodness and beauty; they don't. Trust your sight, not their lack of sight.

They can only perceive neutral facts about Michael (such as how tall he is, the color of his eyes, how he laughs, and the kinds of activities he generally engages in). This information is available to everyone. But you can see more – including Michael's nobility and goodness.

Why do they say 'love is blind'?

As I suggested in my last letter, even on a merely factual level your vision of Michael is more complete, for it includes things others can't know just by looking at him. They must ask to gain this information: where and when he was born, whether he has brothers and sisters, what sort of persons his father and mother are. The closer someone gets to Michael, the more such information he'll gather, but a friend has to be very close – and he must be trusted very deeply – before Michael will reveal his private life, his disillusionments, his joys and hopes, the wounds he's received, his inner self.

Things such as these belong to the intimate sphere in Michael's life, which includes much of his spiritual, psychological, and even physical being. Many things in these areas are so deeply personal that they call for veiling in front of strangers; they're simply private by their nature and should be revealed only in an environment of love, where they'll be treated with reverence and awe.

The closer we get to another person and the more we trust him, the more we desire to know about him, to penetrate his intimate self, and to have him know us in this way as well.

When you fell in love with Michael, you were granted a vision of his true self, the self which he usually hides from others, both because it is his secret and also because he doesn't want to make himself vulnerable to persons who fail to approach him with reverence and love.

It's right to hide oneself from an indiscreet and un-loving gaze, but it's also right to reveal oneself to a person whom we trust and love. This is happening between you and Michael. You now know him better than any other person because he has trusted you enough to reveal himself to you in ways that he's revealed himself to no other human person.

This mutual self-donation is the ideal of marriage and the reason why your love for Michael isn't blind, but is the opposite: it's based on a deeper knowledge and a clearer vision of him than any other person has. Only those who love *see;* and those who see most clearly, love most deeply.

Your special vision of Michael allows you to love him profoundly. Trust this love and nurture it. It will bring you profound joy.

Affectionately yours,

Lily

"I just can't be cheerful in the morning."

Dear Julie,

The French author Balzac writes, "It's easier to be a lover than a husband, because it's easier to say witty things occasionally than to be witty every day."

Balzac is highlighting the fact that an illicit relationship is limited to a short time, when you put on your most attractive face. But marriage is marriage, early in the morning and late at night. This is one of the difficulties all spouses encounter in marriage: they're together when they're not at their best.

As you've discovered, sleeping together is a great and beautiful intimacy; but it also means you wake up together, which for most of us isn't the best moment of the day. We're disheveled, groggy with sleep, not interested in talking, and usually rushing around to get ready for the day's work.

Unless this potentially disillusioning aspect of the intimacy of marriage is counter-balanced by a deepening of your love and spiritual life – and a great measure of patience – it's bound to cause difficulties that don't crop up in a casual relationship.

There are ways to deal with these problems. If you're not cheery in the morning, then talk with Michael about it – but do it later, when you're brighter and more clear-headed. Let him know you're sorry and are trying to change, but aren't having much success. Assure him that in the early morning he just isn't encountering your true self and ask him to avoid discussions at these times, because they're bound to end badly. (Hasn't Michael asked you to do the same for him when he comes home from work tired and grumpy?)

Yes, Balzac is right: it is easier to be a lover than a spouse, because it's easier to be at your best occasionally than to be at your best all the time. But our concern isn't with *what is easier;* our concern is with *what is more beautiful:* a relationship based on the feelings of the moment or a deep enduring love, sealed by marriage, in which the spouses love each other in good times and bad, in sickness and in health, until they're parted by death.

Marriage is the beautiful mystery of *faithful* love – a theme so profound and so fascinating that it unleashes in me a torrent of thoughts which I long to share with you. Your marriage will be blessed because you and Michael see many of the dangers and you're working to avoid them with your love.

Please give my fondest greetings to Michael,

Lily

"So many parties!"

Dear Julie:

You and Michael certainly have been leading a busy social life! I'm glad to see how often you do things together, but be careful not to let that eclipse the deeper dimension of your marriage.

Movies and dinners with friends are enjoyable, but only you two together can develop an *I-Thou* relationship in which you have each other as the exclusive theme of interest. In this special relationship between you and Michael, no third person or object detains your attention: you look at each other, into each other's eyes, into each other's souls, and dwell exclusively in each other's presence.

This deep soul-to-soul relation should be at the heart of your marriage and must continually be deepened and enriched if your love is to grow. I know of many marriages that have grown cold or even failed because involvement with other people or with children has become so predominant that the *I-Thou* dimension has receded completely into the background. The spouses have turned their attention completely away from each other into other activities.

Be careful that this doesn't become a problem for you and Michael. Newlyweds, especially, often engage in such an exhilarating whirlwind of parties and other activities (not to mention jobs) that every night they fall asleep exhausted, but not really closer to each other as persons.

As time goes by, your lives will get even busier (especially when you have children) and there will be more obstacles to the leisurely, sweet intimacy that you now enjoy (and which should be preserved at all costs). So now is the time to develop a deep *I-Thou* relationship between you and Michael, a relationship you'll have to nurture as long as you live.

Your time for each other will gradually grow less, but don't let your lack of time become an excuse for avoiding intimate talks between you. Above all, never let your *I-Thou* encounters become limited to the sexual sphere, which ought always to be a *manifestation* of your spiritual union rather than the only common meeting you ever have.

Success in marriage isn't so much a question of time as of loving longing. Mother Teresa of Calcutta is certainly one of the busiest people on earth, yet she spends hours absorbed in prayer and loving contemplation of our Savior. It is here alone that she finds the spiritual and physical strength to face her crushing duties.

Similarly, throughout your marriage, you should try to reserve moments for you and Michael in which you forget everything else, talk to each other, concentrate exclusively on each other, and revivify your love. In these moments, let Michael and your love for him be your great, all-absorbing theme. These intimate moments will increase your mutual devotion and bring you both deep happiness.

I keep you constantly in my prayers.

Love,

Lily

"I still feel awkward about sex."

Dear Julie,

When you were first drawn to Michael, you called me long-distance to discuss your growing affection for him because its power disturbed you and its meaning was still unclear. While we were on the phone, your little brother entered the room and you asked him to leave until we'd finished talking.

Was that because the topic of love is ugly or shameful? Or was it because you realized that your attraction for Michael was something very intimate, deep, and personal which Bobby couldn't have understood and might even have ridiculed?

You told me that you blushed when Bobby first entered the room; I'm sure you would also blush if you were caught doing something evil. Although outwardly these blushes seem the same, their motivation is quite different: shame is essentially different from what I would call "holy bashfulness." Shame is the proper response to something ugly or evil; holy bashfulness is our response to something beautiful and intimate.

Your love for Michael was by its nature something intimate, which you shared only with those few people you trusted absolutely. So, too, the sexual sphere, which belongs to a very deep layer of your soul, is by its nature very private, and calls for the response of holy bashfulness. Evil deeds *are* shameful; but there is absolutely no shame associated with sexual relations between spouses. Far from it: this union is a beautiful manifestation of spousal love.

Modesty is the virtue which guards the intimate sphere of your sexuality and ensures that it won't be desecrated. Because Michael loves you and you love him – and because you've both sealed your love with the unqualified, lifelong commitment of marriage – it's right for you to invite Michael into this mysterious realm of your soul. Your mutual commitment, rooted in love, gives you the confidence to unveil yourself physically before Michael, knowing that sexually he will bear himself toward you in love.

This physical unveiling is a new act of self-giving, a unique gift that complements and fulfills your earlier psychological and spiritual self-giving. How lovely to unveil yourself to your spouse in whom you have full confidence, saying, "I trust you so completely that I know you will never, ever betray my trust. I trust your generosity and your love."

In this act, there's no shame at all: only goodness, beauty, and nobility. It's akin to giving Michael the key to a beautiful garden of flowers graced with a sublime fragrance. But this garden is to be kept sealed to the public: it is indeed very private, for you and Michael alone.

How deep is my joy for you!

Lily

"I wish it would bring us closer."

Dear Julie,

You're correct in noting that the mysterious sphere of sex doesn't always give what it seems to promise. (That's why immature people, who often equate sex with paradise, are so often disillusioned about sex.)

On the other hand, it would be impossible for you to love Michael and not to desire such a union with him. And yet, you say that sex sometimes separates you and Michael rather than uniting you.

God Himself linked the sexual union in marriage to a profound, ecstatic experience, which is deeply symbolic of the sublime union constituted by marriage. There are various reasons, however, why sex can sometimes lead to disappointment.

First, you must constantly call to mind the fact that in the sexual sphere (as in so many other spheres), joy

26

is a gift, which cannot be claimed as a right or even generally expected. Sometimes, it's given to us; sometimes, it evades us. (The same is true with great music: there are days when listening to Bach's *Saint Matthew's Passion* brings tears to my eyes. On other days, my response is very low-key. I know the music to be equally beautiful in both instances, but fatigue, nervousness, or preoccupation sometimes prevents me from enjoying it fully.)

At such times, patience is called for, so that we can learn always to welcome deep experiences with gratitude, while humbly accepting our apparent failures.

It's also possible that you and Michael have entered the mysterious garden of sex without having first donned your "nuptial garments," that is, without being in that loving, recollected, and yet ardent attitude which is the desirable antiphon of this great experience.

Moreover, since the sin of Adam and Eve, the intense pleasure of sex has given it a powerful attraction in itself, detached from its true meaning as a union of love between spouses, open to procreation. Perhaps the feeling of estrangement you sometimes experience comes from your isolating (however little) the ecstatic experience of sexual relations from your self-donation to Michael, thereby sapping this experience of its profoundest meaning. The less you're concerned about your own responses and the more you concentrate instead on Michael, the better. (Ironically, these kinds of problems can be particularly acute in the first months of marriage when the newly experienced intensity of sexual pleasure may overwhelm one or both of the spouses.)

Unfortunately, even in marriage, spouses can use each other merely to achieve their own sexual satisfaction. Severed in this way from its true meaning and purpose, sex loses its God-given nature as a source of deep joy, and is reduced merely to selfish pleasure-seeking.

Some people even argue that self-gratification is the essential purpose of sex. Happily, they're wrong – very wrong! To view sexuality as merely biological, as an instinct that craves satisfaction, is totally to misunderstand it. Such a view is the opposite of the sublimity of sexual union that is experienced when you are both animated by love, when you seek sexual intimacy not for its pleasure, but as a way of manifesting the deep love which exists between you. At these times, your sexual ecstasy transcends bodily pleasure and includes a genuine joy that springs from the union of your souls deeply delighting in each other.

In such cases, sexuality doesn't serve pleasure; it serves love (and this is its God-given purpose). Even abstinence from sexual relations can serve love. Suppose one of you were sick. To insist on sexual relations would deprive both of you of the deeper dimension of your union: the will to do good to each other. Sexual relations in such circumstances would not be love-*making* but love-*breaking*.

Anyone who has lived an unchaste life and then converts, falls deeply in love, and marries the woman he loves, discovers sex for the first time. He comes to look down in disgust on his earlier promiscuous approach as he realizes with horror that it has cheated him out of one of the most profound experiences human life can give: tender love expressed through bodily self-donation in the permanent union of marriage.

So you see I don't have a puritanical view which judges sex to be evil. Rather I know that an increase of true love between you and Michael will elevate your sexual relations to their most sublime heights. For the essence of your love for each other doesn't lie in sex at all but in your constant concern for the temporal and eternal well-being and happiness of each other – even were that to require a temporary (or, in rare circumstances, even a permanent) abstention from sexual relations.

The Gospel says, "Seek first the Kingdom of God and His justice, and all else will be added unto you." In the same way, the more you and Michael succeed in giving precedence to love, the more beautiful your intimate relations will become. This is achieved by self-giving and self-forgetfulness.

Let your main concern be Michael: his happiness and his welfare. Instead of observing yourself, give yourself. In so doing, you'll find deep joy.

But remember to be patient, too. Sexuality is a turbulent realm, especially for young people. Love will channel these waters, but like all good things, love takes time.

Please write back soon,

Lily

"He cracks his knuckles constantly."

Dear Julie,

Your irritation at Michael's absentminded knuckle-cracking has my sympathy. It's a small thing which it would be best to ignore, but small things sometimes get on our nerves.

(Be grateful that your problems are small: the kind that only get on your nerves but don't shatter love. You've been fortunate to fall in love with a noble man who also loves you, and your union has none of the grave problems – such as brutality or infidelity – that afflict too many marriages.)

Still, even a good marriage has its problems. Now that you're privileged to share in Michael's intimate life, seeing him day and night, you're becoming conscious of many of his odd traits – comical, clumsy, or irritating as they may be. All of us, when examined under the

31

microscope of daily living, reveal quirks of our own that strike others as strange or annoying.

One of my acquaintances had the habit of often scratching his head. One evening his wife remarked to us, "I never knew I was going to be married to an ape." This wasn't a very loving way of regarding his innocuous habit.

It was unkind of her to ridicule her husband (especially in front of others) and it was doubly humiliating since this wound was inflicted by one who had the special mission of nurturing and protecting him.

It could have been otherwise. Marriage constantly offers opportunities which we can use *for* love or *against* love. Michael's knuckle-cracking is just such an opportunity. When you isolate his habit and pay great attention to it, you mentally equate his personality with his mannerisms and begin to view him more as an object than as a person.

It's a bit like taking a picture of someone when he happens to be yawning. During those few seconds, it's true that he looks the way the picture represents him; but the actual yawn which lasts for only the twinkle of an eye has been prolonged by the photograph and therefore deformed and caricatured.

To see anyone "from the outside" is a lack of charity; to see the one you love from the outside is a kind of betrayal. For it belongs to the "pact of love" that you promise Michael (and he promises you) not to isolate single expressions or mannerisms from the totality of the other person – the totality you've seen so clearly in Michael precisely because he's chosen to reveal it to you, and because you love him.

When you suspend your Tabor vision of Michael and look at him from the outside with the critical, unloving attitude of a stranger, the sweet intimacy between you is shattered. You're no longer concerting with him in love; you're conspiring against him.

That's why a lover worthy of the name always strives to look beyond mannerisms and to see her beloved from within, against the background of his lovable personality. Through love's intuition, she grasps her beloved in his depth.

I know you firmly intend to fight against the devastating tendency to see Michael from the outside, and to remain faithful to your Tabor vision of him. The more you succeed in this, the more Michael's minor quirks will lose their irritating character and even grow somewhat endearing to you.

With love,

Lily

"She had no right to ask those questions."

Dear Julie,

Although it's true that we're made for communion, it's also true that closeness between people must be achieved slowly and in stages, as we freely invite others to enter that mysterious spiritual space that is uniquely our own.

Jean's indiscreet questions at the Halloween party attempted too quickly to traverse the space that separates individuals. Like so many people today, she treated you as if you'd been intimate friends for years instead of merely acquaintances of a few weeks.

Today, people do this constantly. Telephone salesmen regularly address me by my first name, which is a sign of an intimacy which I don't have with them!

I'm not just being fussy or clinging irrationally to my European ways; I'm convinced that human happiness

34

depends in part on recognizing this space that naturally separates individuals and on exercising discretion in traversing it.

Recall the development of your love for Michael. Even though you were attracted to him the evening you first met, you still proceeded cautiously in getting to know him and in letting him come to know you. First you asked him about his job and his St. Louis background; then you discussed his interest in hiking and his work tutoring fourth-graders. Only slowly – by concentric circles, as it were – did you (over the weeks) move beyond these "public" areas to come to know his true self: not *what he has* or *what he does*, but *who he is*.

This is how it should be done – much as a symphony develops: the theme is introduced, unfolds, develops, and then reaches a crescendo which has been artfully prepared by the preceding musical themes. (Just imagine how disturbing it would be if the music started with its climax!) Like the themes of a symphony, deep friendship needs time to grow and mature.

You see the same thing in nature: the seed falls to the earth and slowly germinates. Watered by rain, the first shy sprouts emerge, mature under the kiss of the sun, and finally bring forth flowers and fruit. Failure to respect these natural stages of growth can kill a growing friendship as quickly as it can kill a growing plant.

The strength of your marriage to Michael comes in part from the fact that you both have discreetly respected the rhythms of maturation of your love. You didn't skip stages or try to pluck an immature fruit.

By now you've likely noticed that discretion is such an important virtue that it must remain even in marriage. True, you've already achieved a closeness with Michael that would make it hilarious for you to return to your previous reserve and formality. Nonetheless, you remain two separate individuals and there will always be a space between you that must be traversed, however small it may be.

Perhaps Jean's indiscreet questions have highlighted for you the reality of this space, and can now help you better understand some of the points I was making in my last letter. For discretion in marriage is particularly important in sexual relations between spouses, which, like a beautiful symphony, shouldn't move directly to a crescendo, but rather ought to be the culmination of themes lovingly prepared. Loving respect for the stages of development will make your tender encounters with Michael so much more beautiful.

With affection,

Lily

"Physical intimacy can be beautifully spiritual!"

Dear Julie,

Once I was interviewed on the radio by a man who claimed that human beings are just a higher form of animal life. He said there are no essential differences between them and animals. I disagreed, and he challenged me to name one sphere where humans and animals are fundamentally different. Without hesitating, I said, "the sexual sphere." He looked at me with amazement and probably thought me a bit odd.

I was right: although humans and animals have the same bodily needs – food, drink, sleep – the very fact that humans have a soul radically changes the situation. Our body is for us the vehicle through which we can express ourselves, the instrument that sings the music produced by our soul. We can see this difference particularly in the sexual sphere. What a difference there is between the brute satisfaction of the sexual instinct in most animals, and the loving, tender, spiritualized self-donation which takes place in a marriage worthy of the name!

So long as spouses fail to grasp the essentially sublime character of human sexuality, they'll continue to miss the sweet fulfillment that it's meant to give.

But as your mutual love grows and reveals more fully to both of you the profound unity of the human person – body and soul – your experience of the spiritual character of human sexuality will develop into a source of the deepest joy.

I send you both my most affectionate greetings,

Lily

"It really hurt when he said that."

Dear Julie,

You've shown me that dreadful, out-of-focus year-book picture of you, so I can understand Michael's response: "I wouldn't have married that girl!" But I also sympathize with your pain on hearing him say it.

Because of your closeness to Michael, everything he says or does affects you very deeply. When he dropped this remark casually, you heard a nasty interior voice saying, "If he can say that, does he really love me?" Suddenly, all of his many testimonies of love were blotted out of your consciousness. You got stuck on these few words which, to your mind, cast doubt on Michael's claims to love you.

In a way, I'm very happy this happened toward the beginning of your marriage: it gives you the chance to discover how very dangerous it is to take words out of context – divorced from the beautiful story of your mutual love – and to nail your dear husband to his words by insisting: "I don't care how you try to explain it away. You *did* say you wouldn't have married me."

Michael's comment may have meant something very different. His words could also be interpreted to mean, "This yearbook picture is so bad, it has nothing to do with you. I married *you*, not the caricature you're showing me in this picture."

(Don't you like to be told about a bad photograph that it "*doesn't* look like you at all"? It really would be humiliating if someone looked at an ugly picture and said, "It's so typically you; please lend me the negative so I can order a copy.")

Since Michael could have been paying you a compliment, you shouldn't insist on the negative interpretation of his comment that he "wouldn't have married you."

All of us say things in jest or things that are meant to be kind but don't come off properly. We can miss the bull's-eye even with the best intentions. When Michael does this, it's crucial to read his remarks against the total background of your relationship and not to nail him to the literal meaning of his words, holding him responsible for their worst possible meaning. St. Paul's point that "love believeth all things" means that when such ambiguous comments are made, we must believe that what was meant was loving; that is, to use my husband's terminology, we should give our spouse "the credit of love." Love always assumes the best of the beloved, always gives the benefit of the doubt to the beloved.

So try to interpret Michael's statement in a more positive light, and even use it to bring the two of you closer together. In a good moment after you've regained your peace, you can tell him, "You know, I was hurt the other day because I interpreted your comment as a sign of lack of love, but I see that that interpretation was unjustified. I know you love me and I'm glad you love me the way I am now." This explanation will certainly enchant him.

What a joy it is to clear up misunderstandings when you're in love, and to transform a defeat into victory. You'll find that these are the true, lasting victories.

To you both, I send my sincerest affection,

Lily

"We were so glad to see you."

Dear Julie,

How grateful I was to enjoy Thanksgiving dinner with you and Michael while I was travelling through St. Louis! In the gentle and affectionate way that you and Michael looked at each other, I sensed the great reverence you have for each other and I could see how your love has blossomed despite the minor obstacles you both have encountered.

As I said to you at breakfast, even good marriages are sometimes difficult and require great patience and forbearance. Marriage thrusts spouses into such an intimate relationship twenty-four hours a day that small irritations arise in even the best of marriages.

I think, however, that one widespread modern attitude aggravates our difficulties in marriage and in all our other relationships: *lack of reverence.* I don't only mean lack of reverence for God. I also mean lack of reverence for other persons and even for things: the failure to recognize the inner nobility and worth of persons and things which leads to the failure to treat them with the deep, tender respect that is due to them.

In his writings, my husband called reverence "the mother of all virtues" and stressed that reverence is the key to a happy life and certainly the key to a happy marriage. Only the reverent person adopts the right attitude toward his wife, his children, other people, and God.

The irreverent person, on the contrary, approaches others with a basically self-centered attitude. He views the world as a means for his personal satisfaction: "How can these things satisfy my desires?" In doing so, he deprives himself of the greatest and most beautiful things human life can offer, including friendship and love, which are destroyed by the arrogance that forms the heart of lack of reverence.

One of the most ominous symptoms of our contemporary age is its lack of reverence – for people, for sexuality, for the mystery of life, for death, and last but not least, for God. Lack of reverence is so much a part of modern society that we must constantly be on guard lest we, too, unconsciously be infected with it.

We all sin against the dignity of other persons, often in shameful ways. I recall a wife who treated her china with amazing care, while regularly speaking harshly to her husband. There are men who address their bosses with great respect but treat their wives with no reverence at all. "Familiarity breeds contempt," says the proverb. Unfortunately, it contains some truth. It's up to us to falsify it.

Especially after a difficult day at work when you both return home tired and exasperated, it's easy to be testy with your spouse.

Although it's usually difficult in such circumstances, you both must continually remain conscious that your spouse is a person made in God's image and likeness, a being of tremendous dignity, who is to be respected and loved. Continue to show your reverence in the tone of your voice, in your attitudes, in your gestures, in the way you touch each other.

The beauty of your marriage to Michael depends to a large extent upon your enduring reverence for each other. The closer you are to Michael, the more you should tremble with reverence. I personally am convinced that many marriages flounder because there is no reverence between the spouses. No marriage can survive our tempest-tossed existence without it.

My visit with you last week convinces me that you already understand much of this. If you sometimes fail in this domain, the main thing is to acknowledge your failings, ask for forgiveness, and start over again with renewed courage.

To hear from you and to know you're happy would be a joy.

Lovingly,

Lily

"What a moving talk Michael and I had!"

Dear Julie,

How happy I am to learn that you and Michael had a soul-to-soul encounter soon after I left and that since then, your marriage has gained a new glow.

Michael revealed to you wounds he received as a child, but you don't have to apologize for not giving me details about them. (Your comment was sufficient: "To see the wounds of another person is a call to love him more.") The details *should* remain secret between the two of you. Very intimate confidences would be desacralized were they shared with others. Anyway, my role must remain modest compared to your union with Michael. I think you'll find that the closer you become, the less you'll need help from others, for together with Michael you'll be able to resolve the difficulties that arise in your marriage.

What a moving talk Michael and I had!

It seems to me that it belongs to the pact of love that we seal tightly within our soul the secrets that another person has shared with us – all the more so when this self-revelation takes place between two who love each other deeply.

It's true that no one can measure the wounds that spouses can inflict upon each other in the intimacy of marriage. But it's also true that no one can measure the incredible joy and peace that they bestow on each other in a marriage based on complete trust and full intimacy.

Which is why I must again remind you that marriage, like all great things in life, is a risk, a deed of daring. (You'll recall that Plato said that "what is worthwhile is never easy.")

Consider the alternative: a marriage without trust, in which spouses share bed and bank accounts but not their innermost selves. Their bodies are united but not their souls. Even in the most intimate act of all, they remain isolated in themselves. What a horror of loneliness!

So guard well the trust that Michael has placed in you. Let your reverence for him cause you never to reveal his secrets to another and particularly never to use them against him, not even in moments of anger.

Once again, let me tell you how happy I am that a profound communion is developing between you and

Michael. The more you allow yourselves to be refined by love, the more perfect your marriage will become.

Joyfully yours,

Lily

"He's done eating before
I've even sat down."

Dear Julie,

During my visit, I did notice how fast Michael eats and I can understand your irritation when you're left to finish your meal alone. You'll have to pass on to him any of the following remarks that you think would be helpful (and they just *might* be, since in my marriage I had the same problem).

I was never able to compete with my husband when armed with fork and knife. As he was very healthy and had a keen sense for the goodness of food (which he always saw as a gift of God), he always ran ahead of me. Apparently, C.S. Lewis had the same trait: he regularly irritated his hostesses because the food on his plate would vanish before they had a chance to start eating.

That some people have ravenous appetites is something they can't help; others of us eat like birds. In itself, this difference is quite harmless. But in marriage, *everything* is important because the spouses are one. Things that in other circumstances would be morally irrelevant, become morally relevant.

What can you do about Michael gobbling down his food? Remember that Michael has a powerful build while you're like a reed. You can't expect him to become a delicate eater just because he happens to be married to a woman whose appetite is small.

I would try to explain to him that enjoying a leisurely dinner together will increase its delight. But if he can't learn to eat more slowly, I wouldn't reproach him. Instead I'd rejoice over his healthy vitality and certainly not ask him to squelch his appetite.

In marriage, synchronization is always more beautiful than two solos without accompaniment. In fact, one of the major sources of friction in marriage comes from lack of synchronization – not brought about by bad will but by the many natural differences that exist between men and women and by differences in temperament.

Happiness in your marriage depends in part on your recognizing those differences so that you can make allowances for each other. It's always possible for a quick person to slow down but not always possible for the slower to go faster. Because my husband had a far more vigorous physical constitution than I did, he tried to adapt himself to me (although he was not always successful).

This kind of graciousness is one major element in chivalry – that manifestation of love which seems nearly extinct today. Chivalry is based on the principle that the stronger, faster, healthier person should gently curb his energies for the sake of helping the weaker. Consider how slowly mothers have to walk with their toddlers – and how lovingly they do it!

In the same way, with practice you and Michael can learn to synchronize lovingly your differing abilities, needs, and temperaments to form a true union of enduring, complementary love. Not only will your dinners be more pleasant, but your life together will be far happier.

With affection,

Lily

"He came home in a bad mood."

Dear Julie,

Yes, I can well understand what it's like to prepare a nice dinner for your husband and receive in return only a long face and sharp words. Too quickly, the painful questions arise: Is this the same man who once was so loving, so attentive, so grateful? Is this what married life is going to be like?

Hopefully you bit your tongue and refrained from chiding Michael right then, but it's likely he read the disappointment on your face.

To minimize difficulties in situations you've neither caused nor chosen, try to ask, "What is the theme that love offers now?" By *theme* I mean that concern to which you should give your attention at a particular moment. The theme when I'm in church is to adore God; the theme when I take a class is to learn; the theme when

I'm with a beloved person is to concentrate on him, to listen to him, to be receptive to him.

Unfortunately, not only is it often difficult to identify the theme of a situation, but themes also can change rapidly with circumstances. Moreover, we humans tend to be very stiff and stubborn, refusing to give up the theme we have in mind even when circumstances have rendered it no longer appropriate. The true lover, however, learns to perceive the theme of a given situation and act accordingly.

What's the theme when Michael comes home in such a bad mood? Obviously, it's not to feel sorry for yourself and lash out at him. The theme is to try to remedy the situation.

It's clear that Michael, harassed by a rough day at work, was unable to regain his composure while driving home during rush hour. To say the least, he wasn't at his best. (You must have heard the adage, "mediocre people are always at their best." And we both know that Michael isn't mediocre.)

Michael probably came home wishing to be comforted by you, but being upset already, he found it hard simply to acknowledge that he was in need. For some reason, it goes against the grain of many people to admit that they're weak or that they long for comfort. Instead, they tend to grumble, expecting the sweet intuition of their loved ones to understand they need affection even though they act like that's the last thing they want. Realizing this paradoxical way in which people sometimes act, you can see why responding to Michael's bad mood with sharp words would merely cause more trouble.

At first, I would try gently to divert his attention with a loving word or some interesting news. That way you deny oxygen to a beginning conflagration: it will ultimately die out. Drawing attention to Michael's inner turmoil ("How would *you* like to be met at the door by a grouch?") only throws gasoline on the fire.

Later, when he's more recollected, you could inquire about his day and discuss with him those matters that still irritate him. Note how dangerous it is in bad moments to think about yourself: "I've had just as rough a day as Michael and yet I greeted him lovingly. I don't take *my* problems out on *him*." Although this may be true, *it isn't the theme.*

As I said earlier, those who are wise try to recognize the theme and adjust themselves to it: "I happen to be in this particular situation; what am I expected to do now?"

How many unfortunate discussions arise between husband and wife because they don't recognize the theme of the moment. Plain common sense tells us, for instance, that it is unwise to discuss thorny problems on an empty stomach, in moments of great fatigue, or when you're grumpy.

I know that both you and Michael are striving to grow wise. Learning to discern the theme of every situation – whether or when to confront or to comfort each other – will bring you that joyful wisdom which is an outgrowth of love.

Affectionately,

Lily

"We're very merry together."

Dear Julie,

The news that you and Michael have been laughing a lot together makes me very happy. How delightful to engage in witty discussions with a loved one. Paradoxically, the very gravity of your commitment to each other makes real merriment and joviality possible: because you and Michael love each other deeply, you can let down your guard, grow unselfconscious, and laugh and take delight in the shelter of your mutual loving commitment.

But there's a danger here you may not yet have seen. I mention it because – much as I rejoice over the fact that you both love humor and can so heartily laugh together – your laughter must always remain in living contact with your spiritual depths. The superficial level of your soul is ideal for joking and light talk; but only in the soul's depths can serious, valid encounters take place between you and Michael.

In other words, the roots of your marriage go deeper than lovable glee. In marrying Michael, you entered into a profound spiritual relation with him; you abandoned any desire merely to charm or to impress him, and you began an encounter of your two souls in the depths. Spiritually, you chose to stand naked before each other as two persons solemnly dedicated to loving and serving each other until death parts you.

As a result, Julie, you're becoming receptive, eager to listen, and to love both truth and beauty. In your depths, you're growing truly yourself, revealing your interior self to your beloved, and letting him renew and deepen his love for you.

When you and Michael are having fun together – as often you should – these depths of your souls may not for the moment be the theme, but they must never be forgotten or repudiated. When you forget the depth of your love for each other, your innocent humor may easily degenerate into something quite negative: a joking that has a sarcastic tone or a cynical content which can wound deeply.

This corrosive humor isn't genuine merriment. On the contrary, it's a kind of humor which springs from a dangerous superficiality of soul in which we yield to

our moods and act for the moment like amused specta-
tors watching the "zoo" of the world – including our
spouse. We avoid effort, concentration, and responsibility, and too easily say things that we don't mean. Such
moments are a breeding ground for severe disagreements. (I'm sure you've seen parties that started off low
key but grew into vociferous clatter and then ended in
arguments.) Even constant joking can draw us out of
our depths, and once that happens, it's a long and
difficult struggle back.

There's a certain law of gravity at work here, and we
must be aware of it. The secret is never to let our joking
get out of touch with our spiritual depths. (I've always
been struck by the facility with which holy people can
go from recreation to prayer.)

I'm not claiming that marriage should always be
serious and solemn (though it definitely is both). True
love admits much good humor and mirth. I'm merely
suggesting that you be careful to ensure your humor
does not degenerate into something cynical or unloving. Authentic humor always cheers the soul and quick-
ens love.

Love,

Lily

"Sometimes his teasing hurts."

Dear Julie,

After I mailed my letter this morning, I realized that it was incomplete. It's certainly true that when you find your merriment turning into corrosive humor, you should draw back from the brink and ask Michael to do so as well.

But sometimes we don't succeed, especially after a certain point has been reached and our inner peace has been ruptured. (I wish I always had such control over myself that my humor wouldn't hurt those around me or that their joking wouldn't hurt me. Unfortunately, we're weak creatures and I constantly do and suffer things I don't really want.)

When those around me are in a dangerous, superficial mood and cannot break free of it, I find it helpful mentally to put on a protective shield so that whatever is said doesn't affect me. That way I can continue to give them the credit that they truly don't mean what they're saying (which is usually proven true once they return to their depths and – realizing the harshness of their words – apologize for them).

Sometimes love requires us to say (or rather to think), "I know you, and I trust that what you're saying and doing now isn't the true *you* whom I love. So for a while I choose to be blind and deaf, until I have the joy of seeing again the face I know so well and love so deeply." It's a deed of love in such moments to wear armor so the arrows of your loved one (who is in no way being his true self) will bounce back and not wound you.

I'm sure you understand this and I hope you'll be able to practice it, as well. Our insights are valueless when they're not related to our own lives.

With love,

Lily

"We had a great time at the Christmas concert."

Dear Julie,

How delighted I was to hear that you have begun going to concerts together and that in particular you have both come to love Handel's *Messiah*!

What a world music opens for us! When I've been deeply gripped by emotions, I've often had to say, "I just can't express it in words." Music sings what our words would like to say, but can't.

Your shared love of beautiful music is no doubt one of the great blessings of your marriage. That was a gift granted to me, too, in a very extraordinary way because my husband and I had exactly the same love for music, nature, and art, and responded in the same way to beauty.

Sharing an experience with another person deepens the quality of the experience. I feel this bitterly now that

I'm alone. At times, it's almost unbearable to hear one of our beloved pieces of music and to be unable to hold my husband's hand and to look into his eyes.

So I understand your joy: sharing an experience is so much richer and more delightful than merely being in the same room with another person who happens to be performing the same activity as you, but who isn't consciously sharing the experience with you.

If another person happens to look at the same painting I'm looking at in a museum, we're not sharing because we don't intend to have the experience *together*. Our being there at the same time isn't deliberate. It's quite different when you and Michael choose to look at an object together. Then a triangle is formed: the object and the two of you looking at it together. (Perhaps God will grant you the blessing of having a child. If so, you'll experience sharing in a particularly deep way when you and Michael bend over the crib and look at your child together.)

Unfortunately, too few people have ever truly shared experiences with another person, fully conscious of their deliberately having the same experience together, delighting both in the object and in the fact that another is delighting in it with them.

Many spouses live in the same house together and eat at the same table, but have lost a lived-experience of truly sharing their lives and their souls with each other. Most tragic of all, some have given up hope that this is even possible.

Their loneliness must be incomprehensible!

I encourage you, then, to nurture the beautiful sense of communion you have with Michael. What better way to do it than with great music! Plato was right: in its encounter with beauty, the human soul grows wings.

I will keep both of you deeply in my prayers during this holy Christmas season.

Lily

"All this mindless housework!"

Dear Julie,

Yes, I *can* understand why my letter lifted your spirits as you faced a mountain of housework after the holidays. I can also understand how in those circumstances, Betty Friedan's *Feminine Mystique* might seem more appealing than usual, especially her claim that women are bored to death doing housework and caring for children instead of working out in the world. (I imagine that Michael is also somewhat bored fixing things around the house or helping you with the housework.)

For both of you, one thing is certain: if love is no longer the animating spirit behind home activities, they *do* become hopelessly boring. But the same is true of everything else. Typing for pay is boring; you bear it at the office only because you need the money. But like all boring things, it can be transformed if it is done for love.

If you only knew what a privilege it was for me to
type the manuscripts of my husband's books! He, in
turn, often cooked our meals, partially because he was
a great cook when it came to Italian food and I was (and
have remained) a very mediocre one. But while my husband cooked, I helped in the kitchen. It worked out
beautifully, and our collaboration transformed even
the most tedious tasks into joy.

In order for your marriage to be truly happy (and a
successful marriage is always a happy one), everything – absolutely everything you and Michael do –
must be motivated by love and related to the great
human purpose of your life – your marriage to each
other – even when this love isn't felt.

It's so easy for us to forget that *nothing is small for
someone who loves.* Our own mediocrity can make things
small; but if we're animated by love, even our small
deeds grow great with meaning.

So when you face your daily tasks, don't sigh over
their insignificance or grumble about the time they
absorb. See them as little deeds of love. Small deeds in
the kitchen done for love have greater value than a
brilliant Wall Street merger accomplished out of greed.

After all, what is our existence on this earth? A series
of small actions and activities. Few are those whose
lives are dedicated to great things (whatever is meant

by "great"). Most of us must toil by the sweat of our brow, planting, sowing, threshing, cleaning, and repairing...until we die.

This is inescapable, but not a reason for discouragement, for the art of living consists in finding the meaning in these small tasks by relating them to love. This is the secret of marriage (and of sanctity).

You know the great fondness I have for oriental rugs: their patterns, their colors, and their designs fascinate me. It has always amazed me that these masterpieces of creativity are actually made up of tiny bits of wool, lovingly combined.

If someone were to give me many short bits of wool, most likely I would throw them in the wastebasket. What can I do with a few ounces of wool? But a carpet weaver thinks differently. He knows what marvels we can achieve by using small things artfully and lovingly.

Like the oriental carpet weaver, the good wife must be an *artist of love.* She must remember her mission and never waste the little deeds that fill her day – the precious bits of wool she's been given to weave the majestic tapestry of married love.

I'm confident that yours will be very beautiful.

Affectionately,

Lily

"I'm actually happy serving him!"

Dear Julie,

One of the great errors of our time is the idea that service is demeaning. What a catastrophic mistake! Service doesn't jeopardize the absolute metaphysical equality of human beings: male and female are often called to play different instruments in the great symphony of life.

All persons, male or female, have the same human nature and equal dignity. All are made in God's image and likeness; all have a mind, a free will, and a heart capable of loving. All have an immortal soul and are meant to enjoy God forever in eternity.

Unfortunately, the equal dignity of persons is often misinterpreted as identity, i.e., people think it means that "all persons are equal in all things." But equality of dignity is obviously not the same as equality of talents or physical capacity. Just imagine women competing with men in wrestling or in the ring! Men run faster, swim faster, and are physically stronger. (This is why Chesterton claimed that, "There is nothing so certain to lead to inequality as identity.")

Nor does equality of dignity mean that it would be demeaning for one person to serve another. On the contrary, as Plato said, "A man should pride himself more on serving well than on commanding well." Christianity goes even farther by claiming that the essence of greatness lies in service: "He who would be great must be the servant of all." It claims that Christ our King came not to be served but to serve. Meditation on this fact will help you fight the temptation to see housework as degrading service, and Michael as a taskmaster who profits from your subservience. (Remember, too, that Michael serves *you* through his work outside the home as well as by sharing in the household chores.)

These thoughts might help you both to view your work at home and in the office as noble service instead of as an endless round of small, meaningless tasks.

To be forced to serve would be demeaning (though he who forces others to serve, demeans himself far more than he does his servants). But to choose freely to serve others is a sign of love and the triumph of freedom over petty pride.

I'm actually happy serving him!

Think of the mother who cares so lovingly for her child, night and day. Is she a slave, degraded by her service? Or is she, heedless of her own comfort, a model of sublime love made joyful by her difficult service? Like the mother who cares selflessly for her child, the person who loves finds joy in serving his beloved.

I long to hear from you as each of you, according to your particular callings, walk the sweet path of loving service,

Lily

"Who should sweep the floor?"

Dear Julie,

I grant your point that I generally assume that wives will do the housework and that husbands will work outside the home. My assumption doesn't come from any particular prejudice on my part. It's simply an attempt to deal with things as I find them: most husbands and wives live this way.

As I said earlier, in this matter as in so many others, I think you have to try to discern the theme of the situation. You and Michael must determine for yourselves the best division of labor according to your particular talents, temperaments, and circumstances. There are husbands who cook; there are husbands who care for the baby during the night; there are wives who take care of the accounts and pay the bills. Only you two can discover what works best for you.

Still, there will arise new circumstances in which you have to change roles. If Michael falls sick, you may have to work to support the family.

More important than the roles you choose is your mutual willingness to adjust to circumstances (according to the theme that is placed in front of you). To help his beloved, a lover adapts himself to new situations. It is only in very imperfect (and therefore very unhappy) marriages that problems arise from changes in the roles of husband and wife.

Please let me hear from you soon.

Lily

"I want a dishwasher; he wants a stereo."

Dear Julie,

To tell the truth, I'd been expecting this for a while and I'm surprised it wasn't a problem before now. Have you heard about the greedy king who died of starvation because he owned huge amounts of gold, but had no food at all? There seems to be some mystique about money, which goes much deeper than its role as a means for acquiring other things. Is it because money means security (or gives the illusion of security)? Is it because it opens the door to all sorts of enjoyments? Is it because it gives power?

Whatever the cause of the compelling attraction of money, your argument about it with Michael is typical. You want to use your income tax refund to make work at home easier by purchasing a dishwasher and a new toaster. Michael favors spending it on a stereo, elegant restaurants, and expensive wines. "After all," he says, "we have a right to enjoy the fruits of our hard work."

That you and Michael should have different wishes is absolutely normal. I'm convinced that men are usually more pleasure-seeking than women (though when women are addicted to pleasure, they often beat men at the game). And I think that because of their sense for the concrete, women are likely to be more concerned about things that last. As Chesterton jokingly observed, "A duchess may ruin a duke for a diamond necklace; but there is the necklace. A coster may ruin his wife for a pot of beer; and where is the beer?"

Regardless of which categories you and Michael fall into, the question for you both is, "Who is going to win?" In this particular case, you could try to appeal to Michael's chivalry and explain to him that because of your busy schedules, a dishwasher (unpoetic as it is) should be given priority, even though it doesn't deserve to be compared to a stereo which can give keen artistic enjoyment. This approach accomplishes two things: it acknowledges the legitimacy of Michael's wish (which will please him) and hopefully it will convince him to purchase the dishwasher (which would be very helpful to you).

In this case, adequate reasons can be given to resolve the dispute in favor of the dishwasher. But other cases arise in which the reasons on both sides are equally strong. These disagreements are harder to resolve, since each of you will think that his case should carry the day.

To ensure that such disputes don't get out of hand, you and Michael might try now to establish ground rules for resolving future disputes.

One of the key rules, I've found, is that discussions shouldn't take place at the wrong moment – when one of you is tired, pressured, or rushed. It's important to choose a favorable time, when you both are in a loving, recollected mood. Then peacefully discuss the pros and cons of your differing views, seriously trying to understand each other. Don't begin like two duelers whose only aim is to win.

I think you'll be surprised at how quickly disagreements will be resolved if you wait to discuss them in this way in favorable circumstances. In many cases you may both be able to compromise or one of you may give in with the understanding that the next time, the other will give in.

Especially when the arguments on each side are equally weighty and there is no easy way to resolve the issue based on the evidence alone, keep in mind that the person who gives in out of love is always the greater one. This sounds paradoxical, for the winner is usually considered the stronger.

I want a dishwasher; he wants a stereo

But there are two ways of losing. One is out of weakness: the other person has a more powerful will and forces you to yield. The other type of "losing" is in fact a tremendous victory. Think of the mother who gives her child the better portion of food because she loves him! Imagine the husband or wife who gives in, not out of weakness, but out of love. This spouse is by far the stronger one, for he's achieved the most difficult of all victories: conquering his own self-will.

He who truly loves, desires to do good to his beloved. He who wants to "pull the whole blanket to his side" and has very little concern about the other person, is a sorry lover.

This will sometimes mean denying yourself for the sake of a greater good. As Cardinal Newman once wrote, "No two persons perhaps are to be found, however intimate, however congenial in tastes and judgments, however eager to have one heart and one soul, but must deny themselves...much which they like or dislike, if they're to live together happily." Money and most of the other things you may fight about are very insignificant things compared to love. Isn't it a form of madness to endanger the precious gift of marriage over such secondary disagreements?

I'm sure that by now you and your dear Michael have reached a loving solution and have discovered that yielding can be a mark of great strength and that more importantly, yielding is often an act of love.

With all my prayers for you and Michael as the holy feast of Easter approaches, I am,

Affectionately yours,

Lily

"I thought he'd like the plans I made for us."

Dear Julie,

I don't blame Michael for being irked at your response to the Fergusons' dinner invitation for Easter Monday: you answered "yes" without even looking at his face to read his wishes when in fact he was anxious to find an excuse because he doesn't enjoy their company.

It sounds like you've fallen into a common trap – a mistaken idea of oneness in marriage. It's true that marriage is a union of love through which spouses are called to become "one mind, one soul, and one heart."

But there's a right oneness and a wrong oneness. To see the difference, let me borrow from my husband's book, *Metaphysics of the Community*, where he distinguishes between *fusion* and *union*.

Fusion is the melting of two substances into one another. Once fusion has taken place, the individuality of each separate substance has disappeared. Take two pieces of iron, heat them to the melting point, and pour them into a container: they fuse and become indistinguishable because they've become one larger substance.

But this is impossible for persons, who by nature possess such a perfect individuality that they cannot become parts of something else. Moreover, if two persons *could* fuse, they couldn't love each other, because love calls for duality. This is why love between persons aims not at *fusion* (which would destroy love) but at *union*.

Union necessitates that the two persons remain fully themselves, clearly separate – yet bound to each other by "the golden cords of love." A husband and wife who love each other become one, but in so doing, they don't cease to remain fully themselves, two clearly distinct individuals. In fact, mysteriously, through loving union with each other they each find themselves and their own unique individuality in a new and deeper way.

This point may hold the key to the problem you caused by accepting the Fergusons' dinner invitation without consulting Michael. On the strength of your union with Michael, you felt free from the obligation to consult with him. You assumed that because the two of you are one, he would want whatever you want.

Were you to let this become a habit, Michael might come to feel you're no longer taking him seriously as a person – as a unique, irreplaceable individual with his own mind, his own will, his own heart, his own personality – which is the same as concluding that you no longer see him as your beloved partner but merely as an extension of yourself, as if your partnership were a fusion of pieces into one instead of a union of two individuals.

Paradoxically, the closer your union grows and the better you come to know each other, the more you'll both be tempted to take each other's wishes for granted. Simultaneously, it will become ever more important for you to respect absolutely each other's individuality. Remaining constantly alert to Michael as an individual to whom you're united in love will prevent misunderstandings in the future.

Once again, you see that marriage is a constant call to that loving wakefulness in which you "listen" tenderly to another person's soul.

I hope that Michael didn't find your dinner with the Fergusons too painful.

Love,

Lily

"We haven't been as close lately."

Dear Julie,

Plenty of things go wrong in human relationships because the nobler and more valuable things are, the more fragile they are. Fine china is breakable; plastic dishes are not.

As you and Michael achieve a deeper spiritual union, you've begun encountering the unique problems that go along with great closeness to another person. The difficulty with the Fergusons' dinner invitation was one such problem. Sexual intimacy is another. Having experienced the deep joy and beauty of sexual union when it's a manifestation of mature love, you now find anything less than that somewhat disappointing.

In this realm, it's important to be patient with yourself and also with Michael. We're spiritually turbulent beings; our feelings are often out of harmony with our actions. Continue to love Michael and don't fret over disappointments.

May I repeat my constant theme: try to change every defeat into a victory of love. The peace of soul this gives you will smooth the rocky parts of your marriage and intensify the beautiful parts.

With regard to sexual relations in particular, I think it's a great psychological mistake for spouses to enter the mysterious garden of sexual self-giving without any interior preparation. Quite apart from its link with the great event of conceiving a child, your bodily union with Michael in the secret of your intimacy is so great and so mysterious that it calls for an inner preparation. It should be the climax of attention revealed through loving words and loving deeds: a symphony of tenderness manifested in many different ways in the course of the day. (Your heart will teach you what to do.) Then – and only then – will your sexual union acquire its full value as a canticle of love.

Don't misunderstand me. What I have in mind isn't so much a *time* element as a *spiritual* element, for your union isn't merely one of bodies but rather one of hearts *manifested* through your bodies.

Your sexual union is a feast of love, and like every feast, it must be lovingly prepared. This doesn't mean a lack of spontaneity, but rather it gives spontaneity its true meaning. Interior preparation keeps your sexual union from becoming simply a result of habit, an act you fall into as a matter of course. By preserving its true meaning as the sign of two persons in love, you ensure that your marital happiness will grow.

I send you my deepest love,

Lily

"I didn't let him finish."

Dear Julie,

I always marvel that marriages, like souls, can differ so strikingly from each other. Yet your last letter reminds me that marriages, like souls, also have certain traits in common.

Your problem isn't unique: in practically every marriage I know – my own was no exception – husband and wife interrupt each other.

The husband begins a story and his wife cuts in to correct him: "It took place on Tuesday, not Monday, and anyway it was a poodle, not a collie." The story is disrupted, the husband frustrated, and the listeners embarrassed.

Or the wife starts a sentence and the husband, believing he knows what his wife will say, completes it for her while she sits dumbfounded.

To interrupt another person is disrespectful, to say the least, and a polite person wouldn't dream of doing it in formal circumstances. Yet we constantly interrupt those persons who are closest to us. This is the negative side of intimacy, and it has its dangers, foremost of which is irreverence.

It's as if we're so convinced that we can formulate the thought better, we give the other person no chance of completing it himself. Or worse, it's a way of saying: "I already know what you're going to say."

Siegfried Hamburger, my husband's closest friend, had his ear-drum injured during the first World War and later began progressively losing his hearing. The prospect of total deafness troubled him deeply and one day he confided to my husband that he would find it very painful to be cut off from the conversations of his friends.

To console him, my husband promised that when that point came, he would write down for him whatever was of real interest in a conversation. "Thank you so much," retorted Hamburger, "but I would still like to hear your voice – even if you're only saying, 'It's two o'clock.'"

When you're tempted to interrupt Michael, think of Siegfried Hamburger's moving words and realize that one day, if ever you have the great misfortune of being a widow, you'll desperately long to hear Michael's voice – which you've so often silenced.

Maybe this thought will help you to fight our deeply ingrained human tendency to interrupt each other.

Lovingly,

Lily

"He didn't care how I was feeling."

Dear Julie,

What a shame that you've been suffering migraine headaches again! They're so dreadfully painful, yet it's hard for others to be sympathetic since the symptoms aren't outwardly visible.

I'm not really surprised that after your third headache in two weeks, Michael has grown disinterested and even slightly irritated.

But I don't think his reaction indicates that he's callous toward you (even though he's not caring for you nearly as tenderly as you cared for him last month with his bad knee).

If you had something more serious (I don't say more *painful*) than migraine headaches, I'm convinced that Michael would have rallied his love to come to your assistance. Most men lack patience with minor illnesses (whether their own or another's) and don't even like to talk about them.

I agree that your different temperaments lead to a kind of double-standard, with Michael receiving your sympathy when *he's* ill but unable to return it in the same measure when *you're* sick. Perhaps regular acquaintance with bodily discomforts makes illness easier for women to bear and makes sympathy easier for them to receive and to give.

Young men generally aren't afflicted by their bodies, which leads me to believe that the pains and weaknesses imposed by illness do more than incapacitate men; they also humiliate men.

Perhaps this explains their characteristic grumpiness when they're sick – but I still can't figure out why men, who generally claim to be more logical than women, typically refuse to care for themselves properly when they're not well.

But I wouldn't let any of these seeming contradictions become a source of contention between you. It seems to me the wisest thing (besides seeking medical attention when necessary) is to let Michael know how poor you're feeling and ask him to be patient. Then mention the matter as little as possible.

Try not to make of your discomfort a theme repeated incessantly. Because Michael does not understand your longing for tender attention, your complaints probably won't win you more of his sympathy.

Moreover, like many men, he seems simply to be helpless in the face of suffering. I'm sure that with time he'll grow more sensitive to your needs and will learn to communicate his sympathy better.

Know that you have my most loving wishes for a speedy recovery.

Lily

"A lot of little things irritate me."

Dear Julie,

Your difficulties in recent weeks seem to have created for you a problem common not only in marriage, but in life in general.

Outside, springtime is on the verge of turning into a glorious summer but in your heart there's still winter: you've allowed small hurts to pile up and now you suddenly find yourself up against a growing knot of resentment.

Several times these past few weeks, you've clashed with Michael over minor matters; he's snapped back sarcastically. It's hard for anyone to be "awakened" all the time, and the problems you've mentioned indicate that whether because of fatigue or apathy, Michael has definitely not been alert to your feelings. (Have you been alert to his?)

Still, your deep reciprocal love convinces me that you're both well-armed, with God's grace, to overcome these problems which arise in every human relationship, especially if you act quickly each time they arise. Specifically, don't allow your wounds to fester in your soul and poison you against Michael. Taken one by one, they're insignificant. Taken together, they're impressive, even though they're made up of small things. You can deal with one trifle; you can't deal with fifty at once.

One way to keep them from piling up is to discuss them with Michael soon after they occur. That way, you can both work together to find a remedy and prevent future occurrences of the same irritating incidents. And if discussion (in a calm moment, of course) doesn't resolve the problems, then there's still a way – in addition to prayer – that you can work interiorly to ensure that your resentment doesn't build up.

Instead of creating a mental ledger in which you constantly total up Michael's offenses, try to dissolve each one of them in your love as it happens. Every night before you fall asleep, try to consciously put away from you the small difficulties of the day so that you can start the next morning fresh. As St. Paul advises: "Don't let the sun set on your wrath."

No matter how deeply we love someone, human imperfections and difficult circumstances inevitably dull that beauty of soul which we first perceived in him and we come to doubt whether the Tabor vision wasn't simply an illusion which has now fled.

In such moments I turn to the treasure chest of sweet memories I have of the person and I try vividly to recall a word, a gesture, an act of generosity or heroism which has particularly revealed to me his true self, his unique beauty.

As I contemplate his deed with gratitude, our present difficulties recede in importance and my love for him grows strong again.

I've placed many things in my mental treasure chest. One of them is my memory of how a dear friend of mine behaved years ago while we were traveling by plane through a very violent storm. We were both terrified, and I was airsick as well.

When my friend saw how distressed I was, she put her own fear away from her and gently began stroking my hand to comfort me. So great was her tender concern for me that throughout the fearful turbulence, her face expressed nothing but loving kindness.

This touched me so deeply that to this day – even in moments of disagreement with her – I need only recall this episode in order for my heart to melt with gratitude for the gift of her friendship which has illumined my life for so many years.

I'm sure that already you have a number of such beautiful memories of Michael and that as time passes, others can be added. Make a point of remembering them – of putting such memories in your treasure chest. Then, when your Tabor vision of Michael grows dim, run to your treasure chest, recall these sweet memories which you've deliberately placed there, and meditate on them. Your minor disagreements will diminish in importance and you'll soon find yourself able to see Michael again in his full splendor.

Lovingly,

Lily

"Baseball bores me and Michael doesn't like art."

Dear Julie,

That you found the idea of a spiritual treasure chest helpful makes me very happy, but I rejoice even more over your renewed readiness to sacrifice to perfect your love for Michael – even as you're discovering how many sacrifices are called for in marriage.

Sometimes the possibilities for disagreement seem endless. Close as you are to each other, a cause of enjoyment for one of you may be boring or even unpleasant for the other. This is part of the deep drama of marriage: the constant call to "die to yourself" for the sake of your loved one.

You and I love Italian cuisine and, given a choice, we always prefer *spaghetti all'italiana* to hamburgers and french fries. Yet now you often cook American-style food just because Michael loves it. I know you take long walks with Michael when you'd prefer to stay home. I'm sure that to please you, he, too, often gives up a wish, such as going out with his male friends.

I've often found that when I adopt a loving attitude, I can discover in previously boring things the fascination that others find in them. You and Michael might try to learn from each other in this way so that you can come to share more interests.

When you fail, however, the only solution is sacrifice, which doesn't at first seem appealing. Yet it's strange how even seemingly trivial sacrifices can give unexpected joy and nurture love between two people. "God loves a cheerful giver," says St. Paul, so when you do make a sacrifice like going to a baseball game with Michael (Is it such a sacrifice to be with the person you love most?), do it cheerfully so that no one will notice. Advertising sacrifices is a poor way to make them.

The sacrifices I've mentioned so far cause neither of you real harm. It doesn't hurt you to watch baseball, just as it doesn't hurt Michael to go to an art museum with you. There are, however, situations in which one person enjoys something that actually causes harm to another. A case in point is smoking. Suppose Michael smoked, and you (like me) were allergic to smoke: his behavior would hurt you. In such a case, he should give up his pleasure to avoid hurting you, because that must take

absolute precedence over any purely subjective enjoyment he might receive from smoking (which is, of course,
hurting him, too – but I won't speak of that now).

Sometimes sacrifices come from spouses being together; sometimes they come from spouses having to be
apart. I know very happy marriages in which husbands
go fishing while their wives stay home or visit friends.
I also know marriages in which the husband, because
of his ardent love for his wife, doesn't enjoy anything if
she isn't present and would gladly renounce his favorite
activities to be with her. You and Michael will have to
use trial-and-error to find out how sacrifices can best
serve love in your marriage.

You've already taken the most difficult step by realizing that every love calls for sacrifice. And I imagine
you've discovered what a joy it is to sacrifice for the one
you love!

I keep you in my prayers constantly,

Lily

"My plans for the evening were ruined."

Dear Julie,

Your first year of marriage passed quickly! I was so busy this spring that I hardly realized May is almost over already. I apologize for forgetting to send flowers in time for your anniversary, but I'm glad that my phone call helped cheer what in many ways was a disappointing day for you.

As I said on the phone, I sympathize with your distress at Michael's having to bring home an unexpected guest from the office. It ruined the intimacy of your champagne and candlelight dinner and your disappointment endured even though Michael had called in advance to apologize.

How often have I been similarly disappointed when my expectations were dashed by some unforeseen hitch – even though events as they finally unfolded would otherwise have been quite delightful. The disappointment comes not from *what occurred*, but from measuring it against our (often unrealistic) expectations about what we think *ought to have occurred*.

When we dictate interiorly the conditions of our happiness, our very dreams become an enemy. We assume that we have a right to have things go the way we planned and when they don't, we feel that life is cheating us: "I was looking forward to this so much, and now I feel let down."

In such instances, I try to recall the title of C.S. Lewis' book, *Surprised by Joy,* and I try to let myself be surprised by joy. I think you'll find that the deepest and most beautiful moments in your life won't necessarily be those you've planned, but those which are unexpectedly showered upon you like mysterious gifts.

I'm not advocating a defeatist attitude toward life which says, "Don't expect too much; you won't be disappointed." Far from it. Rather, I think we have to try to develop the attitude of a child who gratefully accepts the gifts placed in his path, without constantly making claims. "Unless you become like little children, you shall not enter the kingdom of heaven."

Your experience with your spoiled anniversary dinner shows how dangerous it is to anticipate that an event will happen as you plan it. Clouds often come from nowhere to dash our expectations. So I think we should always hope for the best but we should also humbly accept whatever is given, as God sends it. Whether the sky is cloudy or serene, let's always try to line our experiences with gratitude and sing love's song of praise.

Congratulations once again on your anniversary!

Lily

"I can't understand why he was offended."

Dear Julie,

At first glance, it does seem strange that Michael got upset simply because you said your father could easily fix the radio that had defeated Michael's repair attempts. There must be more to this than you realize. Try to discover *why* Michael was offended – especially since both of you love and admire your father.

No doubt, your relationship with your father has been a great gift in your life. It means much for a young girl to be able to look up to her father. I, for one, owe my own father a great deal. His exceptional reverence for the mystery of conception, child-bearing, and mother-hood will remain with me for life.

But am I wrong in surmising that ever since you met Michael, you've often praised your father at length, perhaps unconsciously holding him up to Michael as a model? These are sheer assumptions on my part, but Michael may have the feeling that you wish he would become more like your father. If this is so, his reaction is understandable. Unconsciously, Michael may assume you love him as a second edition of your father, and that the "author of your days" remains, in your heart and mind, your first love and ideal.

I think it's worth your time to examine whether, in fact, you may have fallen into this error. I call it an error because each of us has his own unique gifts, talents, and callings, as well as his own unique temptations and failings. Our task in this life isn't to imitate others in any absolute way (for we have only one ultimate model: Christ). Rather we must discover who we are meant to become.

We have to judge ourselves not by the standard of another person's personality or accomplishments, but by the possibilities embedded in our own soul. In other words, we should never try simply to imitate others spiritually or otherwise. Each of us is a unique image of God; we can only reach sanctity by fully developing our *own* unique potential as an imitation of God.

I know of a husband who expected his wife to be a duplicate of his sister, a woman of extraordinary charm and talent who combined beauty, intelligence, and great artistic talents. He only succeeded in crushing his wife, who was more modestly endowed. Had he realized what he was doing, he would have been horrified, because he loved her.

You certainly get the picture: if Michael suspects you want him to become another type of person instead of becoming truly himself (which is the deepest longing of love), he's understandably hurt and is right to oppose your expectations.

So try not to compare Michael to your father. Try rather to see the beautiful promise that he has within his own soul and help him daily to make that bright promise a reality.

With my fondest affection,

Lily

"I'm still mad at him."

Dear Julie,

At just the moment when you should be rejoicing that Michael apologized for his sharp words when you praised your father, you're stewing with anger instead. What fickle creatures we are! Our emotional lives are so complicated and we're so rocked by events that it's a wonder our love ever endures.

At all times, but especially now, forgiveness must be woven into the fabric of your love. Your marriage cannot endure without your inner willingness to forgive Michael and to ask him to forgive you for your faults. (This is why the marriage vows also ought to require spouses to promise to ask for forgiveness when they've wronged each other and to grant it when they're asked.)

I remember one of Gabriel Marcel's plays in which a woman justly angry at her unfaithful husband comes to realize that although he's wrong and she's right, "It's not enough to be right." Love requires more: it calls us to forgiveness.

Michael has apologized and asked you to forgive him. How can your heart not be melted by his request?

If you still have difficulties forgiving him, then meditate on the innumerable times you've hurt other people – including those closest to you – and that you've also offended God. Once your heart has melted in contrition, you'll find it not only easy but even a privilege to forgive. And you'll be able to pray from the bottom of your heart: forgive us our trespasses as we forgive those who trespass against us.

The alternative is dreadful. As I've mentioned before, unwillingness to forgive will poison your soul. Too often have I heard the terrible words: "He's hurt me so deeply; I'll never forgive him." Refusal to forgive turns into hatred; hatred becomes poison; and poison brings spiritual death. You won't merely hate; you'll become hateful to others by corroding your own soul.

Love and the readiness to forgive go hand in hand. When you discovered you loved Michael, you understood the need for an unconditional willingness to forgive him – because you love him and you know that your forgiveness is a curative balm for his soul and for yours.

The more you love Michael, the easier it will be to say to him, "Forgive me." The more you love him, the easier it will be to say the words that are sweeter still, "I forgive you."

I'm sure that forgiveness will triumph.

With my deepest prayers for you and your dear Michael, I remain devotedly yours,

Lily

"If only he had listened to me."

Dear Julie,

S o you've fallen into a classical mistake, one I know
well. Of course you were right: Michael shouldn't
have insisted on parking the car in a space that was really
too small for it. Sure enough, he dented the fender.

Michael made the mistake, and even though he was
obviously crestfallen, you aggravated the situation by
repeating those explosively dangerous words, "I told
you so."

Predictably, Michael grew furious. (Next time try to
remember Plato's wise advice never to disgrace another
person, particularly – I would like to add – one who is
close to you.)

No doubt when Michael embarks on a hopeless en-
terprise or is about to make a serious blunder, you must
warn him. But if he ignores your warning, you have to

let him make his own mistakes. Once the error has been made, your theme changes radically: it's definitely not to stress how wise you were to foresee the catastrophe. It's rather to use your gifts to lessen the consequences of the mishap and to help Michael not to lose face. (He should do the same for you when you're the wrong-headed one.)

People are generally very sensitive about the mistakes they've made and it's especially painful if the person they love is the one who rubs them in. Therefore, objectively there's very little sense in ever saying, "I told you so," because by the time you say it, the culprit knows it full well himself.

When discussion of past mistakes is unavoidable, be careful not to preach or insist that you had the answer all along and that he'd better turn to you for advice next time. Think how you would feel if you were in his shoes.

One of the golden rules of marriage (and of life) is "start with yourself." Placing yourself above Michael will always be disastrous, particularly if you appoint yourself as his teacher. Rely instead on the holy contagion of good example, so that your message will come across lovingly and without humiliating your Michael.

With love,

Lily

"But I don't want to humor his pride."

Dear Julie,

I find it interesting that you have difficulty agreeing with my last letter. It shows the amazing power possessed by ideas "in the air." Some feminists have spread the view that women spoil men by protecting their egos, which ought to be deflated instead. I presume these women would recommend that you rub Michael's nose in his mistakes.

Such views are based on the assumption that men and women are essentially rivals and that women suffer because they don't defend themselves. It's about time, they say, that women take the offensive, cut men down to size, and pop the huge balloon of their macho pride.

But do we want war between the sexes, or peace? Do we want hatred or love? Rivalry or complementarity?

Since I approach the problem of love and marriage from a Christian point of view, I have no difficulty opting for the latter alternatives and emphatically rejecting the former. The tragedy of many feminists is that they've totally lost sight of the ideals of peace and reconciliation, grounded in the dignity and complementarity of the sexes.

The moment women compete with men instead of collaborating with them, problems arise. You'll notice that God didn't create Eve to be Adam's rival but to be his companion, which is something very different. So rather than always confronting or judging her friends, a good companion nurtures them.

Sometimes this requires her to look away from their faults – which isn't the same thing as approving those faults or, as you suggest, humoring their pride. Rather, it's merely exercising loving prudence by giving them the space they need to grow out of their weaknesses.

That's why it's all right to refrain from criticizing Michael and it's essential that you not chastise him with harsh feministic rhetoric which too often inflames competition between the sexes, awakening resentment instead of developing cooperation and mutual love.

Please let me know if these remarks help you to bear Michael's faults without anger so that you can work together with him to resolve them.

I don't want to humor his pride

And try to remember to start with yourself.
I keep both of you constantly in my prayers. Please pray for me as well.

With love,

Lily

"Do you mean it's wrong to criticize Michael?"

Dear Julie,

Perhaps I'm having difficulty with this subject because it's so complex and delicate. Let me try a few additional remarks to clarify my earlier points.

There *are* faults which it's not merely legitimate, but even necessary for you to criticize – but only if the time is right and your motives are pure.

First try to discern the gravity of the matter. Ask yourself if it's really a serious matter or merely something that gets on your nerves and that, with a bit of patience, you could learn to put up with.

If it's an objectively serious matter (and not merely a trifle that should be overlooked), then you've still got to purify your motives. Do you recall that St. Augustine said that when he was in Rome prior to his conversion, he was cheated out of money by his students and he hated them for it, "but not with the right hatred." He was more upset about the fact that *he* had been treated unjustly than about the offense to God implied in the injustice.

Try to avoid Augustine's mistake: be sure that your criticisms aren't motivated by the fact that *you* have been hurt, but rather by an objective concern for what is right. In other words, be concerned with the fact that Michael's fault harms him personally (and perhaps others) and also offends God.

Finally, try to choose the right time: if Michael is so tired, nervous, or irritated that any criticism will cause more problems than it solves, then obviously silence is better for the moment.

We should always hesitate to criticize our loved ones, but if it's necessary, we should be sure that we're motivated by a profound and tender concern for their good. Only selfless criticism is loving criticism.

I know that these seem like extremely difficult conditions to impose on yourself, but I've found that when I employ them, I achieve great success. If you save your criticisms for objectively serious matters, ensure that your own motives are pure, and then choose the right time for the discussion, you're far more likely to convince Michael to change his wrong behavior.

And change is what you want, isn't it?

(Of course, my suggestions apply to Michael, as well. He should learn to criticize you only out of love, and when he does, you should try to learn to gratefully accept his reproaches.)

It's surely difficult, but if you vie with each other in becoming more perfect partners in love, you'll rapidly grow closer to God and to each other.

Lovingly,

Lily

"He didn't lift a finger to help."

Dear Julie,

I can't understand why you got irritated when Michael failed to spontaneously help you put the Halloween decorations back into the attic. Why didn't you simply ask for help?

Might there be a subtle stubbornness in you that prefers to suffer rather than ask for assistance? If so, that's unfortunate, because it keeps you from tapping one of the great resources in the hands of women: an appeal to that sense of chivalry that is found deep within the hearts of most men (even though it's often hidden by a thick crust of selfishness).

Of course, it's always a special gift to be with another person who is so alert to your needs that he comes to your assistance spontaneously. But you can't expect Michael always to be that awakened. His inattention and inaction in this case may have resulted from fatigue after a long day instead of from selfishness.

You've often told me that Michael (like all men worthy of the name) is particularly touched when you let him know how much you need him. If I were you I would have said, "Dear, I can't handle these boxes by myself. Please help me with them." I'm sure he would have come to your aid. (I'm not suggesting that you pretend helplessness as a means of manipulating Michael; I simply think that your honest requests for help will provoke a chivalrous response from Michael.)

That's because I'm convinced that although many men seem coarse and uncaring, deep down, most are chivalrous; they feel it's their special mission to help those who are physically less strong – women, elderly people, children. They can be heroic in their desire to rescue someone in need.

Unfortunately, the harsh attitudes of some modern women have badly damaged this noble manly trait. Many modern men have felt the sting of competition from women and have concluded that if women are going to adopt masculine vices (such as aggressiveness, brutality, and coarseness), then chivalry toward women loses all meaning.

Which reminds me of an amusing episode that happened recently in California: a young girl was driving and suddenly had a flat tire. She was incapable of replacing it herself and no one stopped to help her. In exasperation she wrote on a large piece of paper in big letters: "I'm not a feminist!" Within minutes, help came from a young man delighted to be of assistance.

Believe me, you'll always fare well if, instead of competing, you collaborate with men and appeal to their noble, chivalrous character.

Affectionately,

Lily

"I don't worry about dressing well."

Dear Julie,

I know a woman who, while she was engaged, spent a lot of time in front of her mirror to make herself as attractive as possible for her fiancé. Now she's married, and dresses sloppily at home, while making strenuous efforts to be attractive when she goes out.

St. Francis de Sales does tell us that pious women should be well-dressed, but this doesn't mean they must become slaves of fashion. There's a way of dressing which is attractive, even elegant, but at the same time modest and simple. More importantly, attractiveness shouldn't be reserved for guests and those you meet outside the home, while you "let yourself go" when you're alone with Michael.

The moment a couple marries, they should begin to try always to be at their best for each other, physically (and above all) spiritually. Isn't it right that you should give your best to Michael, who has given himself to you in love?

May God bless you and your dear Michael in this Thanksgiving season.

Affectionately,

Lily

"Why shouldn't I just be myself?"

Dear Julie,

Yet another of my letters has failed to convince you! Although I'm trying to grow more recollected for a holy Christmas season, the pressure of practical chores has been so great that I wrote to you in haste and probably did not explain myself as carefully as I should have.

Whatever the reason, you're not convinced, and – if I interpret your letter rightly – you think that always trying to be spiritually at your best for your spouse is artificial, putting on a false front that would strain your relationship with Michael. Many people today think that sincerity requires us to say what we think and show all our moods and feelings so that we are not hypocrites.

I think they misunderstand both hypocrisy and sincerity. For example, just before Thanksgiving I heard a young girl accuse her aunt of being a hypocrite because her aunt made a point of being friendly to a person she disliked. I grant that her aunt's attitude *could* be hypocritical. But was it necessarily? That depends upon her intention, and intentions are best known to the person who has them.

Let me be more specific: suppose that I strongly dislike someone, but I'm particularly sugary toward him either because I need him for something or I want to appear very holy. This is, indeed, being hypocritical. But suppose that, realizing how subjective and unkind my attitude is, I try to go to my depths and see this person as a child of God endowed with an immortal soul. As a result, although my dislike of him hasn't gone away, I nonetheless greet him lovingly.

In this instance, I'm far from being hypocritical. On the contrary, I've collaborated with my deeper self, transcending my own aversion in order to try to see the person as God sees him. This is true charity – not based on fleeting feelings of sympathy but on awareness of the person and his sublime value as a child of God.

I know someone who believes she's very honest because she wouldn't hesitate to tell you that you dress badly or that you have a crooked tooth which ruins your smile. This isn't honesty, but plain rudeness: the manifestation of superficial feelings which hurt others.

Instead, we should deliberately return to our depths where we can bear ourselves toward others with the kindness and respect that is due to them. Be wary of believing that because you happen to have a particular feeling or thought, honesty requires you to express it.

So, when I urge you and Michael to be spiritually at your best at all times in your married life, I'm not advocating a "hypocritical phoniness" (as you put it) that would cut off spontaneity. Rather, I'm asking you to distinguish between your deeper, valid feelings and your more superficial, invalid ones, and then, by means of your free will, to sanction and embrace fully the valid feelings and reject those which are invalid.

Your illegitimate feelings may not disappear, but at least they can't take root in you because they haven't been nourished. Hopefully they'll soon wither and die, particularly if you continue to reject them when they crop up again.

Be faithful to the beautiful Tabor vision of Michael I spoke of in my earlier letters. I know that this is sometimes difficult and that the Tabor vision – first given as a gift – must continually be revitalized.

This is to be expected. The Apostles saw Christ transfigured on Mount Tabor, yet they, too, had to return to the foot of the mountain and later re-ascend, sometimes through fog and rain, sustained only by their faith that the now-obscured vision remained true and that Christ still awaited them at the top.

I'm sure that there are similar moments when the vision you were once granted of Michael seems to be only an exhilarating illusion that was mistaken for a valid reality. This is where your faithfulness grows important. In faith, you must hold fast to your original vision of Michael, even though faith may now have to replace sight. Together with God's grace, your vision retained in faith will give you the strength to go forward, to ascend steep rocks, to face the dangers and difficulties. The promise of recapturing the beauty you once perceived will give you wings and strength.

Here your will is most important, for any authentic love must be confirmed by many acts of the will which sustain us when – for whatever reason – our feelings wane.

So when you love, love Michael as you saw him clearly in that first vision. Then you'll always want to give him your best, as a special gift to him. (It's always a source of suffering for a lover to realize that he's unable to give his beloved the best of everything, including the best of himself. But at least, let's give all we can and pray soon to be able to give more.)

I hope this convinces you that I'm not recommending artificiality, but rather fidelity to your true self.

Especially in this Christmas season, we are called to a profound recollection of soul which transforms our attitudes and actions with love.

I will pray deeply for you and Michael as we joyfully celebrate the birth of our Savior.

Lily

"It was a serious fight."

Dear Julie,

Yes, it does sometimes amaze me that disagreements over such small matters can take place even between people who, like you and Michael, agree about most of the major issues in life. I'm sure that some of the blame should be placed on your hectic holiday pace. Michael's vacation was really too brief for you to drive to New Jersey the day after Christmas, be in Chicago three days later, and then return to St. Louis New Year's Day. Exhaustion shortens tempers.

Yet it's clear from your comments that fatigue is only part of the reason for your fight. Differences between your individual desires and temperaments contribute to the difficulties as well.

But I'm convinced that you're also having problems that are nourished by the perennial tension that exists between men and women, beings who have very different structures and viewpoints, and who therefore often attach a different importance to things. Exhaustion and tension always accentuate the effects of these differences but I don't think they are insurmountable.

As the Bible teaches, man and woman were created as complementary beings, who are intended to enrich one another through their different structures and their common love in ways that simply aren't possible between beings of the same sex.

Neither of you can bring forth a child alone; together you can become parents. This fruitfulness is reflected in your souls as well, and all that you engage in together is richer because of it. This is precisely what happens in a happy marriage.

Then why does your nature sometimes clash so strikingly with Michael's? I believe that the problem originated with Adam and Eve. When they sinned against God together, they became estranged from Him. Their sin also divided them *from each other* in a profound way. (Sinning together always ultimately separates partners in sin, which is one facet of their punishment.)

Both male and female natures were deeply affected by original sin. All the remarkable male qualities of strength, courage, and nobility were sapped at their very roots. You've probably noticed that when angered, a young boy's first reaction is to use his fists. Like most men, Michael must struggle against the temptation to let his strength degenerate into brutality, his courage into rashness, and his nobility into haughtiness and pride.

And surely you've experienced parallel temptations: your natural sensitivity threatens to become merely self-centered sentimentalism and your attention to detail can quickly turn into pettiness. (At such times, I'm sure that Michael is tempted to sing with Higgins in *My Fair Lady:* "Why can't a woman be more like a man?")

Throughout these recent months, you and Michael have been encountering the effects of the Fall of Adam and Eve on your differing natures, which were really meant to be in harmony, not conflict. In moments of stress, Michael loses sight of the beautiful secret of womanhood which you embody, and you in turn lose sight of the manly strength and nobility which he embodies. You seem to falsely identify each other not with *who* you are, but with your characteristic weaknesses. This is far from the divine plan God had when He gave Eve to Adam and when He allowed you and Michael to give yourself to each other.

You can look upon this fallen situation as a tragedy (which it is) or as a challenge (which it also is). As I've said before, Christian marriage is a high calling: the ideal setting for re-establishing the original harmony between man and woman so badly disrupted by sin.

What an ambition for you and Michael – noble and difficult! But with humility, perseverance, and prayer, your love will triumph.

With all my good wishes for a New Year filled with reconciliation and love,

I am yours affectionately,

Lily

"He gets mad when I say 'always.'"

Dear Julie,

Just when matters were being patched up between the two of you, you shattered the peace with that word which seems so innocuous but which, in fact, is loaded: *always*. You can use it about insignificant things ("You *always* leave the towels on the floor") or you can employ it in much deeper accusations and reproaches ("You *always* treat your mother better than you treat me").

And like its twin (*never*), *always* always causes problems – problems that can be avoided.

Not only is it unfortunate to say *always* when you really mean *often* or even *sometimes*; it's a failure to acknowledge that Michael has often done the right thing without your noticing it or at least he's put up a courageous fight to do so but has been defeated. How quick we are to notice failures but not victories!

Emphasizing Michael's failings can discourage him, especially if serious matters are involved. Proclaiming loudly that Michael *always* falls into a weakness (like being fearfully impatient) when, in fact, he might be trying hard to avoid it, may lead him to a dreadful conclusion: "Whether I try to improve myself or not makes no difference as far as Julie is concerned. I give up."

How much more loving it is to refrain from showing your annoyance or at least to use the occasion also to compliment Michael for the real progress he's made: "You've been so good about hanging up the towels lately that I was surprised to find them on the floor this morning."

The spirit of love fills this statement, taking it out of the realm of cold judgment. We must always be careful to bear ourselves toward our spouse in love, so that our differences with him won't become obstacles but will help him on his way to perfection.

If we always do this, then *always* and *never* will no longer cause problems in marriage, and even things which annoy us will help us grow closer together.

Let me hear from you again soon,

Lily

"It's so hard to change."

Dear Julie,

The first time I met my husband, he was giving a talk to a group of friends in his modest apartment on Central Park West. His theme was "the readiness to change," which is also the first chapter of his great work, *Transformation in Christ.*

I can't tell you the impression his lecture made on me. For the first time in my life, I discovered the key to moral and spiritual progress: *the readiness to change.* I left his lecture in a state of exhilaration and gratitude that hasn't faded from my memory to this day.

But life was to teach me that having a key isn't the same as being able to use it properly. As a matter of fact, when I look back on my life, I see that lack of readiness to change has marred much of my spiritual development.

In a sense, we all seem to be "old maids" – people who've never adapted ourselves to living with others. We have set ways and a horror of changing ourselves (along with a passion to change others). I know people who take insignificant details so seriously that a spoon placed in the wrong drawer causes a sort of earthquake.

Even in marriage, most of us implicitly consider "our way" to be the best way. When we're challenged to change, our first reaction is often, "That's my business" or "Leave me alone" or "I'm a free person and I've got a right to do things as I choose." It's strange how very, very difficult it is for us poor human beings to change even in the smallest things. (Obviously, I'm referring to changes for the better. We should never yield to our loved one's will to do evil – that wouldn't be love but mere weakness.)

It's difficult for us to change for the better because readiness to change means fighting our own will. This is a great source of conflict in marriage. Much as we would like to be great lovers, we must acknowledge that we love our own will more. We love God – up to a point; we love our husband – up to a point. But as Kierkegaard noted, our most dearly beloved usually is and remains our own will.

One thing alone brings people to the readiness to change: love. Love can melt the coldest heart, making it fluid and malleable. What a liberation from self-imprisonment to be able to go against our own wishes out of love! Love makes dying to my will sweet, though it may be that this sweetness is enjoyed only after a long struggle.

Your love for Michael is great, and so is his love for you. So I don't doubt that you both will rise to the challenge of love and soon learn how always to be ready to change for your beloved.

With my fondest affection,

Lily

"Maybe I should quit my job."

Dear Julie,

You're confronting a difficult dilemma about working, especially as it becomes harder for you to juggle the demands of marriage and your both having a job. It's a struggle shared by too many working women today. How will you pay the bills if only Michael works? Yet how can both of you continue to work and still have a decent family life?

It's not a question of whether women should work, for women have always worked – and how! Raising children and keeping house is truly work. But the social changes of the last few decades mean that women are now competing with men outside the home, sometimes in positions previously reserved to men.

You asked whether wives should work outside the home. I can't answer with a definite *yes* or *no*. It all depends on the woman's concrete situation, on the calling Christ is placing before her as an individual woman. In a word, it depends on the theme that is presented to her.

In our society, the overwhelming majority of childless wives work. In principle, I have nothing against it. Indeed, I myself spent thirty-six years as a college professor, so I know both the benefits and the problems of professional women.

Some women simply must work: their husbands are ailing, unemployed, or don't earn enough. But others seek careers because they hate housework and prefer to leave their home and children in the hands of others rather than do it themselves. (Ironically, they usually wind up working in an office all day and then have to come home and do the housework, too.)

Work outside the home can be flashier, more exciting: you feel in the midst of things, with life pulsating around you. You earn a salary which, to many people, means success and accomplishment.

However, along with these benefits come problems. I'm sure that by now you and Michael are fully conscious of the chief of them: your job can become the central theme of your life. I know from experience that it's very difficult to work full-time and keep marriage absolutely and completely in the foreground where it belongs. In the work force, questions of competition, promotion, and professional success clamor for first place.

This is a good time for you and Michael to try to clarify your priorities and to realize that even if you must work to make ends meet, your relationship to each other (and later to any children you may have) should be the human core of your hearts. Using this standard, you'll be able to gauge whether your working is doing more harm than good, and then you and Michael can choose accordingly.

With all my love,

Lily

"Michael walked in at a bad time."

Dear Julie,

We human beings are strange creatures. When we dine with the president of the company, we carefully prepare ourselves for the encounter, reviewing what we will say and how we will say it. We foresee difficulties; we brace ourselves for problems.

This is appropriate; our career is at stake.

And yet, after a long day's separation, when we're about to see again the most important person in our life, we rarely prepare ourselves at all. We walk into the house assuming we can just "come as we are."

This is a grievous mistake.

We should always prepare ourselves for our time with our spouse at home. As we discussed earlier, I'm not recommending a false front, but rather a deliberate recollection of soul, a few moments of meditation in which you call to mind the precious gift of love and of your marriage to Michael.

Especially since it was Valentine's Day, you assumed as a matter of fact that when Michael returned from work, he would greet you radiantly and express his joy at finally being with you after long hours at work.

It turned out otherwise.

Michael was tense, exhausted, and very much in need of the warm atmosphere of a loving home. He also had assumed (too readily!) that he would find you in the most peaceful of dispositions, yet your day at the office had also had its problems and irritations.

Had you both recollected yourselves for your meeting, you would both have been ready to respond to your failed expectations with loving understanding. Instead, you each rushed in expecting love and consolation – not irritation – and when full, sympathetic attention wasn't paid to your own problems, you each reacted to your disappointment by striking out verbally.

Instead of home being the solace and refuge you each needed, it became as unpleasant as the rest of the world had been. The evening was ruined.

Next time, try to recollect yourself before greeting Michael and ask him to try to do the same. I'm sure you'll both be delighted by the difference this makes in your marriage.

I look forward to hearing from you again soon. In the meantime, please extend my warmest greetings to your dear Michael.

Lily

"Should we bring our problems home from work?"

Dear Julie,

There are people who become so involved in their work that they never let go of it. Even at home, they're physically present but spiritually absent because they're still thinking about their job: they have eyes and do not see, ears and do not hear – which is very hard on their family.

This is one major threat that work poses to your marriage. So when it's the theme for you to be with each other (or with anyone else, for that matter), push your work-related concerns out of your consciousness and concentrate on the person before you: his words, his concerns, his needs. Listen to him and try to make sure that you're truly present to him.

Some time ago, I read a very touching story about a man who accomplished this in a very unusual way.

Should we bring problems home from work?

Most evenings before entering his house, he stopped at a bush just outside the door and pretended to place in it an invisible package containing his cares and worries from work. In this way, he symbolically left his problems outside (I would say, "in God's hands") so they wouldn't disrupt his family life and burden his young children. As he left for work again each morning, he would pretend to pick up his package again, and only then would he let himself begin worrying about his problems.

Apparently, on those evenings when he left his problems outside the door, this businessman thought that bringing them into his home wasn't the theme. Like him, you both should try to discern the theme of the evening – whether it is prudent to bring up important problems or to defer them for a better moment. (I emphasize the word *important*, because you should do your best never to burden each other with little irritations.)

Sometimes it's best to leave your worries at work; other times it's essential that you share them with each other so they can be borne more easily. As always, use discretion to discover the theme: What is Michael's state and what is yours? Are either of you so tired, agitated, or discouraged that business problems would aggravate an already tense situation? Would they ruin the precious hours you have with each other? Or would your failure to talk about them leave you in such inner turmoil that even worse harm would be done?

You'll have to answer those questions yourselves at the time, and should be prepared to have the answers differ from day to day. So long as you're sensitive to the theme placed before you at the moment, I think you'll do well in deciding whether at any particular time it's best to bring your troubles home from work or to leave them on a bush outside the house.

With love,

Lily

"I'm putting in a lot of overtime."

Dear Julie,

That your job has become so burdensome grieves me, and I imagine that this early spring weather makes it even more burdensome by contrast.

It's obvious that work is very much on your mind, and I understand how you must suffer when you come home exhausted after long hours at the office, only to find that shopping still needs to be done – and then comes cooking, dishwashing, and the rest of it. It becomes easy to forget that the meal you share with Michael is one of the most important times of your day.

No wonder you came home the other night wishing you could just gulp down a sandwich by yourself, and relax. It's surely difficult to make Michael realize you're happy to be with him when, in fact, you're harassed, harried, and fatigued by the bustle of professional life.

It's a daily struggle for a working spouse (whether husband or wife) to keep marriage in the center of life. Even if you succeed theoretically, you may fail practically because of the constant demands of professional life.

There will always be emergencies at work, times when you're called on to give more than what is strictly required. At such times, it's especially easy to begin to do things at home carelessly.

Yet if you do keep your heart in your marriage, you soon find that colleagues who don't share your wise sense of priorities run ahead of you, because they're willing to sacrifice their personal life for their job. You can tell that their heart and soul is in their work, not their family life. Their profession is their god.

I always gave highest priority to my marriage, but the consequences for my career were enormous. I was constantly reminded that greater dedication to the college (which usually meant tedious committee work) would greatly enhance my chances of promotion. I was a career woman who gave first place to my husband, but it wasn't easy. (However, with hindsight I can tell you how happy I am that I gave our marriage precedence.)

I'm not advising you to do your job carelessly. Far from it. The moment you're at the office, your theme must be to perform your assigned tasks with all your concentration and talents.

Rather I'm addressing the question I raised in my letter to you last month: should work be the center of your lives? Should it be rated higher than your marriage in your list of priorities?

Without fixing the answer firmly in your mind, it's going to be hard (on a day-to-day basis) to keep your priorities straight.

I know some women who solved the difficulty by abandoning their dream of a successful career and giving themselves fully to their families. Now as they look back on their lives, they don't regret the choice they made. When the tension between their professional duties and their family responsibilities grew too great, they had the wisdom to sacrifice their job to their vocation.

How beautiful to have a husband devotedly attached to his wife, a husband who recognizes she has been the great gift of his life! How beautiful to have children who love and respect their parents and have admirably developed their talents!

This is the great reward of spouses who've discovered that love is the greatest of all vocations. In one of his later books, Malcolm Muggeridge captured the thought exactly: "All I can claim to have learned is that the only happiness is love, which is attained by giving, not receiving."

I send you both all my affection,

Lily

"Our marriage just hasn't been the same lately."

Dear Julie,

Your recent letters haven't been very cheerful. After nearly two years of married life, somehow things don't seem as luminous as when you first fell in love. I suspect the problem is that you two have grown used to living together. The glamor of novelty, the tremendous adventure of sharing the intimacy of another person's life has worn off and you've slowly settled down into routines.

Your engagement was a happy time: you had spiritual wings; you radiated joy and gratitude; you were fully awakened. No effort was too great; no problem scared you. How your heart used to beat fast at the thought of seeing Michael! Now you're more concerned about whether he'll come home early and dinner won't be ready.

Yet, your marriage should be even more beautiful than your engagement period. If that weren't so, then why should people get married at all?

In the time since your wedding, you and Michael have gotten used to being together. It's *normal*; it's what you expect; and therefore it's no longer so thrilling and heart-warming.

You both seem to have slipped into a state of spiritual sleepiness. You're taking things for granted and are no longer grateful for the gifts you've received. Like a worm creeping its way into an apple, habit has crept into your marriage.

I'm sure you've found that habit is a tremendous danger that menaces not only marriage, but all great things of life. Habit is even more dangerous for having many good points. As a sort of second nature, it enables us to do many things easily and with a minimum of attention. (Imagine how difficult driving would be if you constantly had to make an effort to remember what to do next: which pedal to press, when to shift gears, and so on.)

But desirable as habits are in practical life, they can be disastrous in marriage. When you're ruled by habit, you make the same gestures and you accomplish the same tasks – but they're empty because you aren't fully attentive as you do them.

146

Being with others calls for constant alertness, wakefulness, presence. You know how frustrating it is when you're with another person and you have the feeling he's somewhere else. Even if he says "yes," "uh-huh," "right," these seem to be just mechanical words.

I'm convinced that habit is one of the greatest threats to marriage. It's like a gray dust that powders everything, taking away its glow and beauty.

I'm a widow and have always hated spiritual habits; and yet when I look back on my own life, I have every reason to cry over the inroads this spiritual disease made in my marriage. How many times, I recall now, I took things for granted and no longer experienced them with the grateful alertness typical of true love.

Unless you wage war against habit, your marriage will be caught in its deadly web. Daily, you should try to shake off spiritual habits and realize anew what a tremendous gift your marriage to Michael is, how you pined for it, how impatient you were, how despondent you were when you feared it would never be granted to you.

Now, God has given you this gift. Like a flower that must be watered every day, water your love for Michael with gratitude and recollection. Thank God for it, and promise you'll tenderly care for this fragile plant with great attention. Think for a moment how terrible it would be to lose your beloved through death; imagine how you would regret your present spiritual sleepiness.

I'm sure that with Michael's help, you can free yourself from the deadly web of habit and make each day a time in which you can lift up your heart in gratitude to God for the great gift of Michael and your marriage to him.

As Kierkegaard put it, "in heaven, there will be no habit." And surely, marriage is meant to be an anteroom of heaven.

With all my love,

Lily

"He's been hard to live with this week."

Dear Julie,

What a bad week you had! I'm also sorry to hear that Michael has been distant and irritable. Recently, things really haven't gone very well for you. So I can understand why today my words about your special Tabor vision of Michael sound hollow and my praise of the beauty of marriage seems unrealistic.

Your remarks remind me of some of the criticisms of my husband's book, *Marriage: the Mystery of Faithful Love*. Some people said that it proposes an ideal of marriage so high that it's unattainable: a fairy tale vision, a book for newlyweds only. Worse (they've said), his praise of the greatness of marriage might lead couples to believe that there are few difficulties in marriage. This could cause them to grow too quickly discouraged when troubles arise and to conclude that their love was an illusion in the first place and that their marriage isn't worth saving.

What a catastrophic mistake this would be! Our imperfections follow us wherever we go, even into our marriage, beautiful as it may be. Only sheer wishful thinking could believe that the moment a person marries with a heart full of love, all his faults – his pride, self-centeredness, willfulness, and mediocrity – would evaporate.

We're very imperfect human beings. The older I get, the more I find that "without Christ, we can do nothing." Much as you and Michael long for love – much as you're made for love – conflicts can arise in your marriage with amazing speed. It was inevitable that you'd soon find you're very poor lovers when it comes to living love, day in and day out, winter and summer.

Next Friday is Good Friday, the day the Church commemorates Christ's death on the Cross. After Christ's crucifixion, the Apostles suffered days of desolation because Christ's mission seemed to have ended in complete defeat. But how could Peter, James, and John forget Christ's transfiguration on Mount Tabor which had revealed to them His divinity?

Like the apostles after the crucifixion, you're presently experiencing darkness, which is inevitable in marriage. The crucial thing at such times is to call to mind the glorious Tabor vision of Michael granted to you in your moment of falling in love. What you saw then, even though it might seem an illusion now, was the true Michael. Your Tabor vision was a valid insight, not a figment of your imagination.

Suppose you hadn't originally been given this vision which enkindled your love for Michael; and suppose you didn't also have a sublime ideal of marriage. If that were the case, why should you sacrifice for it now? Why fight for something not worth fighting for?

As I said earlier, some people criticized my husband's book because it proposes such a high ideal of marriage.

They were wrong.

Only extremely high ideals about marriage will enable couples to get through the hard times. When the sea is rough, it's doubly important for the captain to keep his eyes fixed on the lighthouse marking the safe harbor. The beauty and greatness of marriage should be your constant beacon, precisely because you're still so far from shore.

Your fidelity to the ideals of love and marriage will give you and Michael the courage and strength to triumph. If you abandon these ideals, how will your love survive? A mediocre view of marriage leads to a mediocre marriage – and mediocrity dooms marriage.

How many Wall Street brokers are willing to work feverishly all night long for the sake of making a few more miserable dollars! Shouldn't you be willing to make even greater efforts to save, deepen, and improve the most important thing (humanly speaking) that you have: your love for each other? How wrong are the defeatists who anticipate problems and disappointments so much that they approach marriage like an ascetic exercise that simply must be endured!

Marriage is worth fighting for – and no sacrifice, no effort should be considered too great to achieve the noble goal of a perfect union between spouses.

Once Michael's irritableness has blown over, I'm sure I won't have to convince you of this. Right now, the important thing is to fix this goal so firmly in your mind that you never let it be dislodged, not even by the gravest misunderstandings. Especially in this holy season, remember that the darkness of Good Friday was soon followed by the glorious, saving light of the Resurrection on Easter morning.

Likewise, prayer, patience, and faithful, tender love will carry your marriage through these dark moments to the beautiful light shining on the other side.

Much love to you and your dear one,

Lily

"Their marriage seems so perfect."

Dear Julie,

Just this morning I received your letter telling how you and Michael are depressed about the luncheon you had with the DeLisles. How ironic that a pleasant afternoon with friends can turn into an occasion for distress. Their very joy with each other upsets both of you, because – and I admire your honesty in admitting it – you envy them.

They seem to have achieved what very few couples achieve: perfect harmony, a synchronization which reminds you of a perfect duet. Suddenly all the small, daily annoyances and arguments which arise in your marriage sallied into broad daylight, and you saw how far you and Michael still are from perfect unity. This doesn't surprise me. Don't forget that not all marriages have exactly the same difficulties. Some human beings have easy and pleasant temperaments (Christine has one of the gentlest dispositions I've ever come across, which is a big help in a marriage). You and Michael aren't as mild-mannered – but neither are you at war with yourselves from morning to night, which would also make marriage very difficult.

So perhaps you should ask, "What's the theme for you and Michael now?" And consider your distressing luncheon as another situation giving you the choice between the right or the wrong response. The wrong response would be to drop your arms in discouragement: "Maybe others can do it – they were dealt a better hand. It's just no use with us." The right response is to let George and Christine's beautiful marriage convince you that true harmony between spouses is in fact actually achievable.

When you get discouraged, try to recall the story of St. Augustine, who, before he converted, heard about the wondrous deeds Christians had accomplished and exclaimed, "If others can do it, why not I?" And he struggled still more courageously, with God's grace, to free himself from sin.

No doubt, your marriage can be improved in many ways. But this fact is actually far less important than your continuing resolve to pick yourselves up after every fall and declare, "Now we're starting once again."

An imperfect married couple who continually strive to deepen their harmony and love is far better off than a couple who believe they've reached perfection and settle down in complacent smugness. I'm sure that George and Christine didn't achieve their unity overnight or without great sacrifice and suffering. As in any great love-relationship, unity came from their steady will to keep improving and it will only continue so long as they maintain that resolve.

Regardless of the particular difficulties that afflict your marriage, loving patience, good will, and prayer (a lot of prayer!) will enable you to triumph over them, provided you both truly desire victory – which I know you do.

Let the example of George and Christine lead you and Michael to practice even more ardently "the art of loving." The beauty you see in another garden is a call for you to tend your own with greater love and care.

With deepest affection,

Lily

"Maybe I criticize him too much."

Dear Julie,

Although it may be hard for you to realize amid all your struggles and trials, there are unmistakable signs that the love between you and Michael is deepening.

One of these signs is that you've begun to take an honest and objective look at your own faults instead of concentrating primarily on Michael's.

It's funny how easy it is to notice the defects of others, while gleefully overlooking our own. One reason for this is that our attention is more easily directed to things outside of us. But the deeper reason is that to know ourselves is a very painful process.

The danger of narcissism is deeply rooted in all of us. It's such a marvelous feeling to think of myself as an exceptional person: attractive, graceful, witty, intelligent, talented, winning! It's easy to fall comfortably into all sorts of illusions about myself.

My defects tarnish this image. Is it any wonder I try to look the other way? I prefer to concentrate on the faults of others, which don't pain me at all (except when I happen to be their victims).

You've noticed quite a few imperfections in the one you love. I'm not speaking about things Michael can't change – like the shape of his nose – but things that lie in his power. You find him lazy, impetuous, prone to lose his temper, and so on.

Rather than discussing these problems calmly with Michael to help him to improve, you've caught yourself habitually pointing them out and indicating you would appreciate his changing them.

When you give vent to your criticism in this way, not only do you achieve very little, but Michael retaliates by vehemently pointing out your own faults (such as your quickness in criticizing him). It usually degenerates into an argument.

Thank God, you've begun to change these defeats into victories (and you know, I'm sure, that the greatest victories are conquests over defeats). You're learning an important lesson about life and particularly about married life: we must start with ourselves. (If only revolutionaries and terrorists realized this!)

The strange thing is that in starting by reforming ourselves, quite often we bring about unexpected solutions to problems. We discover that our own thoughtless actions were provoking the bad reactions that we deplored in others. And we find that our new virtues make it easier for others to change.

Our great example in this regard is St. Monica.

She had a callous and irascible husband, but instead of trying to curb his temper with criticism and with reproaches – which would only have increased his aggravation – she overcame her own temper and learned patience.

This brought about two results.

First, in contrast to her friends' husbands, Patricius never became violent with her, which made it easier for her to continue to try to love him properly.

Second, Monica's example of goodness finally won Patricius over, so much so that she had the joy of seeing this pagan enter the Church shortly before his death.

She had turned her primary attention away from *his* faults to her own, and worked on becoming more holy herself. She saw that it was far better to concentrate on the weeds in her own garden before tearing up his. She had discovered what successful preachers and missionaries always find: saintliness is more effective than eloquence.

Maybe I criticize him too much

Like St. Monica, you have many reasons to be hope-
ful and encouraged. And your eagerness to perfect your
love for Michael gives me continuing joy.

        With my warmest affection,

Lily

"I asked him to forgive me."

Dear Julie,

How happy I was to hear that you've put humility into practice, asking Michael to forgive you for being so critical of him. And how beautiful that your humility not only touched him deeply, but led him to acknowledge his own weaknesses.

As the French poet Theophile Gautier wrote, "Pride quits the human heart the moment love enters it." Love is the sun which melts the ice of our pride and enables us to say, "I was wrong. Please forgive me."

I just wanted to tell you that your letter gave me a special joy. I think that things will soon begin growing better in your marriage.

With love,

Lily

"He forgot our anniversary!"

Dear Julie,

From your letter, I gather that you were offended last week when Michael forgot your second anniversary – a day that means so much to you, a day written with golden letters in your heart and memory. He didn't greet you in the morning with "Darling, this is a great day for both of us!"; he asked whether you had remembered to cancel his dental appointment.

I must confess that I felt like laughing when I read your report of this. *My Fair Lady* came to mind again. Do you recall Professor Higgins' tirade against women and his question addressed to his friend Pickering: "If I forgot your silly birthday, would you fuss?"

As you might expect, Pickering (like most men) said he wouldn't. You see that Michael isn't the only man who has "sinned" by forgetting an important date. Like

Michael, most men remember little things like taking out the garbage but forget momentous events like anniversaries. (Some men forget to take out the garbage!)

That you got married is as important to Michael as it is to you, but that it was on Friday the 21st of May is a fact that strikes him as somewhat irrelevant. I know that these days a lot of people would disagree with me, but I'm convinced that this is just a result of the obviously different psychological rhythms of men and women.

As a woman, you have a strong sense for the concrete – a particular date, a particular hour. Michael, on the other hand, is more abstract, which is why your attention to detail may sometimes get on his nerves. I'm sure he often wonders to himself, "How can she be so particular? Who cares whether the table is set just right? Concerns like that are petty."

It's my experience that modern couples who deny the reality of these fundamental psychological differences have more problems than do those couples who acknowledge them and lovingly use them to enrich each other and their marriages, putting into practice the mutual complementarity I mentioned before. One of the marvelous and challenging things about marriage is precisely this invitation to transcend your own structure and to try to understand your spouse and to grow better as a person with him.

Consider, for example, your feminine sense for time and details. No doubt, you see something important in times and dates, but you may also tend to get bogged down in these time-concerns and too easily fault Michael for unfaithfulness to the past if he happens to overlook them.

Michael should also learn to transcend his own male structure and to realize that your concrete touch is a strength, instead of dismissing it as a "typical female mania." Paradoxically, the more he understands your vision of things (*the female vision,* you might say), the more you'll be able to put it in the right perspective. At the same time, he'll learn to pay more attention to details and to be sensitive to your concerns.

There are countless other areas where you and Michael can enrich each other. Michael seems to share the natural male talent for severing his mind from his emotions, whereas you have a beautiful meld of heart and mind, precisely one of woman's most admirable characteristics.

Attentiveness to Michael's virtues will help you to incorporate into your female character certain "male" traits like objectivity, broadness of views, and courage – without thereby becoming masculine. In turn, Michael's loving attention to you will help him to replace his typical male abstraction and coldness with compassion and sensitivity to others. He won't become effeminate; rather his character as a human person will mature.

As you each incorporate the qualities of the other sex in your own structure, you'll become more human in the Biblical fullness of this term (for "God made man; male and female He made them"). You can see this in the great saints. Recall the gentleness and sweetness of St. Francis of Assisi, the boldness and strength of St. Catherine of Siena and St. Teresa of Avila.

What a blessing it is when, through the person you love, you are able to transcend your limited, narrow view of things! Learn to approach each other as the blind man approached Christ: say tenderly to Michael, "I long to see!" Then, the next time he forgets an anniversary, remember it's not a sign of lack of love but rather of natural male/female differences. As you learn more about each other's psychological structures, I'm sure such problems will diminish in frequency.

With my most joyful love,

Lily

"I'm trying to understand his point of view."

Dear Julie,

Your letter touches precisely on what I meant about how men and women can enrich each other. You could have lost your temper because Michael was indifferent to the mountain of practical problems you faced in preparing for your mother's visit. Instead, you suppressed your anxiety and didn't insist on immediate action but rather tried to see things from his less troubled perspective, which allowed both of you room to deal with the situation calmly and realistically. Your loving reaction also probably helped Michael be more responsive to your legitimate concerns, and to give the problems the quick attention they needed.

You're both learning to rely on the better traits of the other, while not succumbing to your own characteristic weaknesses. Instead of squabbling, you each took a step toward the other. Michael caught himself before he ran out the door, and stopped to listen and show you his sincere concern about your troubles. And you didn't raise your voice, nag, or burden him unnecessarily because you remembered your love for him.

You're becoming more womanly and Michael more manly.

How marvelous is this mutual enrichment of man and woman! It is – if properly understood and lived – so enriching that you could say the differences between the sexes are truly a very special divine invention. I encourage you to keep on teaching each other to see more.

Ever yours,

Lily

"I'm teaching him to be sensitive."

Dear Julie,

The mail is slow these days, but I still hope this letter reaches you before you leave for your Memorial Day camping trip, especially since I think I expressed myself poorly in the letter I mailed this morning.

I believe I ended by saying that you should "teach each other to see more." I'm bothered by the word *teach*, because considering yourself Michael's teacher could be catastrophic for your marriage.

As you've found, marriage *is* a school of character; but the great teacher in marriage is love, not either one of the spouses disguised as a schoolteacher.

Love Michael and help him to love you – but never appoint yourself as Michael's teacher or think that it's your mission in life to change, correct, improve, or educate him. I don't mean to exclude all criticism; I

167

simply mean that you mustn't set yourself over Michael as his teacher (or vice versa), for this would destroy the precious equality that makes spousal love possible and it would cause your marriage to begin to crumble.

I keep you always in my thoughts and prayers,

Lily

"Why doesn't he say 'I love you' more often?"

Dear Julie,

Please don't be too upset at Michael for thinking that his helping to do the household chores sufficiently demonstrates his love. Most men are surprised when their wives expect them frequently to say, "I love you."

It's not that such husbands don't love; it's that they feel their actions speak louder than their words and that therefore declaring their love is unnecessary. "After all," they argue, "when we were dating, my declarations of love were necessary to convince you. Now you're convinced: we're married. So why should I repeat what I've already convinced you of? Listen to my deeds."

This logic would be persuasive if the words *I love you* were meant merely to convey information. Fortunately, they aren't. They're meant for something far deeper:

they manifest a love that calls for repeated manifesta-tion. In this way, they keep their full, virginal value every time they're repeated.

Gently let Michael know that just as his deeds should continually reveal his love for you, so should his words. Declarations of love can't be too frequent. Repetition has a deep meaning in music and in life, and marriage in particular should be a symphony of love.

With deep affection,

Lily

"I've decided to work only part time."

Dear Julie,

D espite the difficulties it will cause, I'm glad you've decided to cut down your outside activities and take only a part-time job. This allows you to continue to earn money – which young couples usually need – while letting you create for both of you a home which will be your place of rest, the place where you both experience love.

I realize this was a difficult choice and you're still unsure of its wisdom, but be encouraged, for you'll soon discover that many hidden joys lie in the trials such a decision brings on.

A deepening of your love for Michael will be your reward for giving up many of the extra conveniences and pleasures that your full-time salary was providing. You know how empty and short-lived is the happiness that purchased things promise! Now you may be poorer – in terms of money – but you're infinitely richer in each other because you'll have more of the time with each other that love needs to thrive.

I'm convinced that you're about to experience in a new way the profound joy that marriage can bring.

With much love,

Lily

"He's been so wrapped up in his work."

Dear Julie,

You seem worried that Michael is so absorbed by his job that he only comes home to relax between hours at the office. It's a common problem, probably more noticeable now that you're working only part time.

Many men are tempted to gauge themselves according to their professional success and can easily become depressed when they feel they're a failure at work. Moreover, as I've mentioned before, they're very conscious of the responsibility to support their family and easily believe that when they've done that, they've met the demands of duty, and can relax.

This is laudable but it also contains a subtle danger: namely, that work may become the center of their lives and home the place where obligations cease and they're entitled to take it easy.

At work Michael finds challenges, excitement, and novelty; he can exercise his talents and creativity. But deep down, like all human beings, he longs for something else, something infinitely deeper: love.

I suspect our world is so noisy in order to cover up our spiritual and psychological emptiness, to help us forget how sad we are. Behind the facade of loud music and the rush and clamor, there yawns the immense sadness of lives that have no transcendent purpose. How many people are there who don't know (and don't even seek) the meaning of life? How many people are there who've never met someone who truly loves them and who enables them to rejoice over the fact that they exist?

You must constantly call to mind the importance of your role as spouse. No doubt it has its worries and tedious chores which often seem petty or boring. This is one reason why radical feminists decry marriage as a jail in which male totalitarianism has imprisoned "the second sex."

But they leave out the essential: woman's true mission to create a place of love and joy – which no one can find in professional work. Humans aren't machines; they're persons. No one who realizes the nature of personhood can limit his horizon to exterior activities.

As wife, you must collaborate with Michael in setting the spiritual tone; you must be a fire that warms those who come close to you. In a good home, all members of the family feel sheltered in the sweet knowledge that they're loved and understood; they can put down their defenses.

The more you succeed in helping to create this atmosphere, the more Michael will long to come home. He'll realize that – absorbing and satisfying as it may be – success at his job pales in comparison to the loving warmth of home and the joy of the communion of souls he experiences with you at home.

So try not to be disturbed by Michael's long days at work, and never fail to praise him for his accomplishments.

Persist in your love and love will triumph. (It always does.)

I send you all of my affection.

Lily

"He made such a big deal out of it."

Dear Julie,

You probably remember my description of marriage as that human relationship in which things that are *in themselves* morally irrelevant become morally relevant: love endows everything with importance.

Michael's anger at your being half-an-hour late is a case in point. Since you weren't responsible for the long lines at the bank or the traffic jam by the park, Michael's irritation was clearly out of proportion to your fault. (I'm sure that this dreadful summer heat made things worse for him, but also remember that Michael is an extremely punctual person and tends to see lateness as not only a lack of courtesy, but even a lack of love.)

However, regardless of how exaggerated his reaction was, once you saw his anger, you should have apologized rather than defending yourself and exclaiming,

"Michael, you're making a big deal out of nothing!" Your statement was guaranteed to provoke him further and lead him to accuse *you* of never being on time, which understandably angers you, too.

Peace comes only when we're primarily concerned about our own faults, not those of others. There's nothing more upsetting than being accused yourself when you have legitimately reproached someone else. And there's nothing more disarming than hearing someone say, "Yes, you're right. Forgive me. I'll try to do better from now on."

Lateness and a thousand other irritations will work to separate you from Michael. In marriage, such frictions are unavoidable, which is why the ever-present theme of marriage must be love. It's love that will lead you to avoid doing things that irk Michael. And when irksome things happen anyway, love will cause you to hasten to apologize, to assure your worrying loved-one that it couldn't have been helped, and to add how much you regret having caused him concern.

Michael's own apology after he calmed down is evidence that although (like you) he still has occasional lapses, he's growing in humility and forgiveness, which are essential elements in every enduring love.

So I wouldn't be very troubled by small setbacks such as this spat about your tardiness. Minor problems remain, but I think that so long as you both retain your good will, you'll be able to transform all of your good (as well as your bad) experiences into gifts of great value for each other — because they're filled with your mutual love.

Affectionately,

Lily

"I can't ignore all of his faults."

Dear Julie,

Your response to my last letter makes me wonder if I expressed myself adequately on one point. I do think it's best to apologize when you're wrong and to silently bear with Michael's occasional lapses; I don't, however, think you should remain silent about habitual faults which Michael *could* correct. They're not good for you, for Michael, or for your marriage.

You love Michael and love always strives for the perfection of the beloved. Yet Michael can't change wrong behavior he doesn't realize is wrong. So beware of falling into brooding or resentment about faults he may not realize he has. You need to forgive him; but you must also, somehow – without nagging, preaching, or strife – gently bring to his attention those faults that may be obvious to you but not at all obvious to him. Wait for a quiet moment, and then tenderly discuss with him those problems that must be overcome if your marriage is to flourish.

Often people say that love is blind. How foolish! As I've mentioned before, it's not love that's blind, but hatred. *Only love sees.*

When you fell in love with Michael, you saw both his good points and his bad, and you rightly concluded, "The goodness I see is clearly *his true self* — the person he's meant to be. I know that despite the faults that mar his personality, he's fundamentally good." (Isn't that just the judgment that's implied in your last letter when you said, "When he gives in to his anger, he's just not himself.")

Notice that your judgment involves not merely a recognition of Michael's virtues, but also a grasp of his weaknesses and flaws. Which is why I say that love isn't blind; it actually sharpens our gaze. (God, who loves us infinitely, sees our goodness as well as every single dark spot that stains our souls.)

People who hate can no longer see the good points of a person. They too quickly judge that "the evil I see in this person is his true self; he's bad through and through." You love Michael, but you also can't help but suffer from his faults and imperfections. What should you do about them? One thing is certain: to close your eyes to his defects, and claim that you love him so much that you see only goodness in him, wouldn't be true love but plain illusion. The opposite mistake — because you see his flaws so clearly — would be suddenly to grow so impatient with his faults that you forget his true self and lose hope that he'll ever change.

St. Paul tells us that it's the strict duty of the lover to believe that, in spite of difficulties and delays, his beloved will achieve victory. Whether in marriage, in education, or in giving advice, the moment we say to another person, "I give up — you'll never change," we place a huge stumbling block in his path to improvement. On the contrary, your loving belief that Michael will achieve victory in his own good time will give him the most powerful incentive to improve himself.

Finally, try to beware of over-reacting against Michael's shortcomings because they make *you* suffer. In other words, oppose his faults because they offend God and hurt Michael, not because they get on your nerves and you "can't take it any more." As you know well, it's amazing how sensitive Michael is when your criticism is motivated by selfish reasons. On the other hand, when he knows your criticism springs from tender love for him, it makes a great impression on him. The more selfless you are in opposing Michael's faults, the better your chances are of helping him overcome them.

Once again, you're discovering how very difficult it is to love truly and completely. It calls for such delicacy of feelings, such hearkening to another's soul, such selfless concern for his good, that we need God's constant help to reach that goal.

Your experience in marriage shows you that it would be unwise to expect to reach it in just a few months, but you can draw closer every day. Michael's temper will no doubt continue to upset you and make you suffer. But try at those times, lovingly and patiently, to meditate on the selflessness of true love which, as St. Paul says, is "patient and kind, is not jealous or boastful, is not arrogant or rude, does not insist on its own way, is not irritable or resentful, does not rejoice at wrong, but rejoices in the right."

What a program St. Paul proposes! Certainly it's difficult — all great things are difficult — but with God's help, great things are also possible. Again I say, be thankful even for this difficulty. If such sublime virtues weren't called for in marriage, would any of us voluntarily take the steps necessary to acquire them?

With affection,

Lily

"Michael's colleague cares only about money."

Dear Julie,

Despite the inherent difficulties, I'm convinced that a marriage between two persons deeply in love is the greatest earthly source of human happiness. I feel sorry for Michael's colleague who seems to expect happiness from money. Success, money, and power are typical modern substitutes for the great, noble good of a love-communion with another human being in marriage.

But they're poor substitutes, and I wonder if people finally turn to them because they despair of reaching the heights. Like Dante when he strayed from the right path, most men "abandon all hope of the ascent."

Haven't you yourself sometimes been drawn toward substitutes for love? Your recent concerns about the house being decorated just right and about becoming a perfect hostess could also develop into substitutes for that happiness in marriage that comes from deepening your union with Michael.

You've turned to these concerns partly to occupy yourself now that you're only working part-time, but your letters suggest that you've also grown somewhat passionate about these tasks. Could your mutual forgetfulness of the real depth of your love have led both you and Michael to give more time and attention to other activities, and less time and attention to each other?

Remember how beautiful it is to stand with another facing the world. That's the reality of your love, which remains today, even when it's somewhat hidden behind your daily activities.

A student of mine once claimed that if she had a cigarette and a glass of beer, she was perfectly happy. Obviously my dear student had confused being *satisfied* with being *happy*. Worse, however, than this common confusion is the fact that seeking mediocre pleasures inclines a person toward a life without grandeur or love.

Compare this attitude with that of St. Thérèse of Lisieux, who speaks of the "immensity of her desires." Your great desire to strengthen your marriage shows you're already far along the way toward achieving it.

Contentment with ourselves condemns us to mediocrity; likewise, contentment with a mediocre marriage

condemns *it* to mediocrity. A deep longing for a beautiful marriage — tempered by patience and good will —
will lift your marriage to ever more sublime heights as
time goes by.

There you'll discover a wealth incomparably greater
than that of Michael's colleague or of anyone else who
fails to recognize the greatness of the gift of love.

I'll pray that God will reawaken in your soul the
keenness of your love for Michael and will grace your
marriage with all His richest blessings.

Please write soon,

Lily

"Our intimate life is growing stale."

Dear Julie,

One of the great dangers today is to set up a wrong alternative: work or fun. Most people come home so exhausted that they have only one wish: to put up their feet and relax (which usually means watching television). But this alternative (work versus fun) leaves out the essential: our relationship with persons – first and foremost with God, but then also with the persons we love. How sad and impoverished is a life in which slaving and relaxing are the only poles of our existence.

I must repeat what I said previously: since you're now at home more than Michael, you should try to make of your home a place where it is good to be, where your exhausted husband will discover that the blessed relaxation of your common love is infinitely more gratifying than a silly television show.

In too many marriages, the husband is so absorbed in his career that he pays less and less attention to his wife. (Unfortunately, today many working wives are becoming similarly absorbed in their work.)

In such marriages, one unfortunate consequence is that the only time the husbands look at their wives is in the bedroom. They view physical intimacy as a relaxation which enables them to work better the next day.

Finally, the relationship between such spouses is reduced to watching TV and sleeping together. ("My husband just wants to sleep with me. Other than that, he has no interest in me at all.")

What a tragic impoverishment of human life and a maiming of marriage! I could cry over this destruction of the beautiful relationship that is meant to exist between husband and wife. Although your own marriage hasn't fallen into such a terrible state, I get the sense from your last letter that you find yourself slipping in that fatal direction.

Many people take it for granted that such a dreadful relationship is the best that can be expected from marriage – but don't let this terrible despair afflict you.

Tenderness, loving interest, and profound spiritual concern must characterize all relations between you and Michael. Rededicate yourselves to the exchanges of views that used to animate both of you. At dinner, talk with Michael about what happened in the course of the day. Share your successes and defeats, ask advice, read to each other. Now that the fierce heat of summer is waning, take walks together holding hands and enjoy once again the beauty of togetherness. Believe me, once Michael gets over his initial embarrassment, he'll be charmed by this special attention and will eagerly come to you for more.

Your role as wife calls for you to set the spiritual tone. Like most men, Michael simply can't do it. He's so immersed in his work at the office that he brings that atmosphere home with him and finds it hard to enter into the tender intimacy of the home unless he's actively drawn there by you.

As wife, you must take the initiative. Once you do, I think you'll make the sweet discovery that what seems unfair to some people today is, in fact, a special privilege granted to women.

Your moments of spiritual intimacy with Michael will then form the background for your acts of bodily self-giving. They'll restore to your sexual experiences their true character as an expression of mutual love. And joy will once again permeate your marriage.

With my faithful affection,

Lily

"Should I love him just to get him home?"

Dear Julie

No, I didn't mean to imply that you should use love simply *as a means* to lure Michael back home. That wouldn't be love. And anyway, love isn't a *means* to anything. It's something to be desired for itself and given freely for itself.

Love is essential in the life of every human person. In fact, I had just mailed my last letter when I recalled a remark by a former student of mine. We were discussing love when she said, "When I'm loved, I feel real."

I don't know if she realized how deep her remark was. Of course, I praised her, but the more I thought about it, the more I became convinced that she had made a very important point.

When a baby is cared for materially but not loved — if no one looks at him, cuddles him, kisses him, or makes him feel like a welcome guest in this world — he never develops normally. Each baby develops his own unique individuality through this loving relationship to his parents.

Just so, all persons develop their full individuality through loving relationships with other persons and with God. These loving relationships bring about a spiritual blossoming for which there is no substitute. Perhaps this is why it's true that when we're loved, we feel real.

A friend of mine told me how he once stepped into a taxi in New York and greeted the driver with, "Good afternoon." Deeply moved by this, the driver turned to him and said, "I've been driving a cab in New York for fifteen years, and you're the first person who has greeted me."

What a condemnation of our society! What a lack of reverence it is to view a human being exclusively as a means to an end.

Too many people have never met someone who truly loves them and who enables them to rejoice over the fact that they exist. How dreadful it must be for all those who feel unreal because no one greets them, rejoices at their coming, regrets their going, or even notices them! There are too many such living "unmarked tombs"; too many people who live and die anonymously.

Should I love him to get him home?

If they're atheists, their fate is worst of all, for they believe that when they die, they fall from this loveless world into stark nothingness. But if they believe in God and know there is Someone who cares for them and loves them infinitely, they feel real in spite of the human indifference that surrounds them.

My husband was loved very much by simple people, whether at the food store or at the college when he chose to accompany me. He always — and I mean *always* — greeted people, from presidents to elevator operators, with a hearty "good morning" or "good afternoon."

These might seem to be small things: they're not. However important we may be in the worldly sense, it must never blind us to the human persons we're dealing with.

This applies particularly in marriage.

How important it is for you to be at all times conscious that Michael is a human person, and vice versa. How very important it will be in your relationship with your future children to exercise authority over them, yet to be full of reverence for their personalities.

So rather than loving Michael in order to get him home, love him for who he is. Return again and again to the treasure chest of your precious memories and recall with gratitude the gift of Michael and of your love for him.

By Love Refined

As you renew your devotion to him each day, I'm confident that you'll see the love between you begin to blossom once again.

God bless both of you,

Lily

"I thought I knew how to love."

Dear Julie,

Your sorrow over your faults distresses me when I consider only its negative side. It's indeed painful for you to think that in difficult times, you've let your beloved down in many ways, and you've failed to love him as he deserves.

But there's a positive side, as well.

Many people feel they're morally impeccable because they've never murdered someone or robbed a bank. Their spiritual and moral horizons stop right there.

However, the more we love, the more sensitive we become even to our small failings which, though normally imperceptible, become strikingly visible under the magnifying glass of our love for another. How many opportunities do we miss to say the right word or to foresee another person's difficulty and help him when he totters?

He who truly loves discovers that his love is imperfect and laments the fact; he would like it to be powerful as a torrent, clear as pure water, ardent like fire, tender as a soft breeze. In fact, only when love reaches a supernatural level, a partaking in Christ's love, does it become "what it wants to be."

That you're disillusioned about the flaws in your love for Michael simply indicates that you've grown in self-knowledge. When you married Michael two-and-a-half years ago, you thought you were capable of great love — someone for whom love would always be the most important thing in life. You thought you would always be willing to give up everything for love.

Now you know from experience that to live your love isn't an easy thing. How tempting it is to take Michael for granted, to demand instead of to give, to dictate how he should behave toward you while resenting even his minor criticisms (however just) of you.

Try to consider your new self-knowledge as a reason for hope. How many illusions we have about ourselves: how easy to imagine we're heroic, selfless, generous, and humble; how painful to discover we're far — very far — from having the noble virtues we aspire to! Yet true self-knowledge and reform require us to face this fact.

Haven't you noticed the profound link between love and humility? Love is grand and glorious, but it's lined with humility. You can be a mathematical genius and be very proud; you can have an iron will and be very proud; but you can't love and be proud.

Love teaches humility.

Now your discovery of your imperfections has left you humbler, but it's no reason for the despair you mention. You can't cultivate a deeper love if you fall into despair about your capacity for loving.

Isn't despair as much a wrong response as was your confidence in your ability to love without limits? In fact, both are animated by pride: just as you judged yourself a great lover (and really weren't), so you mustn't judge yourself a cold and proud woman, incapable of loving anyone. You're neither — and to think that you are is to go from one pitfall to another.

Instead, use this humbling discovery as an occasion to acknowledge your weakness, and try, with God's help, to learn to love better. A good swimmer doesn't let himself be overpowered by a violent wave; he uses it to his advantage.

Your painful discovery of your imperfections can similarly be used for your sanctification and for the perfection of your marriage. All of life should be a school of love.

Julie, you're growing day by day. You now see clearly things that were spiritually invisible to you just a few short months ago. To my mind, this is a sign of great progress. Don't lose sight of the fact that your yearning for goodness endures despite your failings.

Be confident that with Michael's help and God's, your love for each other will grow into that sublime communion to which all married couples are called. When Christ cured a possessed boy, He asked the boy's father, "Do you believe?" And the father responded, "Yes, I believe. Help my unbelief!" Similarly, you and Michael must say to each other, "Yes, I love; help my lack of love!"

With best regards and my constant affection,

Lily

"I'm learning to forgive myself."

Dear Julie,

Your letter made me quite happy. I've the feeling that you grasped the gist of the thoughts in my last letter even though they were imperfectly expressed. You immediately opposed the wave of depression that was overpowering you and changed a defeat into a victory.

Yes, I'm sure God forgives the selfishness that continually creeps into your marriage — that self-seeking garbed as love which you detect more and more. God always forgives us when we're contrite. (Recall the words of the Psalm: "A broken and contrite heart, O God, thou wilt not despise.")

His divine grace will help you to achieve that marvelous and necessary balance between recognizing yourself as a sinner and respecting yourself as a child of God, made in His image. It's a spiritual tightrope we must

197

walk, and yet so long as we persevere, it can be done, because God is there to help us.

With love,

Lily

"I've been trying to pray more."

Dear Julie,

Your new longing for a deeper spiritual life gives me great joy. I see that you've begun to realize its importance for your marriage. The closer you come to God, the more you'll be able to love and the more beautiful your marriage will grow.

In your characteristic way, you've thrown yourself into your "new life" with ardor and enthusiasm, which is certainly praiseworthy. Indeed, prayer and spiritual reading will help you enormously to solve your daily difficulties in the light of Christ. You'll quickly discover that your struggles have been shared by innumerable souls who achieved victory because they relied on Him who works best in weak vessels.

But at the same time, I think you'll soon discover that just as your imperfections followed you into marriage, so they'll follow you into your new-found religious enthusiasm and might even sometimes lead you to do harmful things in the name of religion. The problem won't be your new-found relation to God, but your old failings as a person.

So it's wise to be prudent in your enthusiasm; don't force your new religious devotion upon Michael or judge him if he balks at joining you: God alone can judge. Remember that everyone has his own rhythm of development and it wouldn't be right to expect Michael to follow yours. Not all flowers bloom simultaneously.

You intimate that Michael has already made a couple of half-humorous, half-sarcastic remarks about your new dedication to prayer ("I didn't know I was going to marry a nun"). Perhaps he fears he may be shoved aside if God comes to play a central role in your life.

Of course, true love of God doesn't diminish our love for other persons. Just the opposite: the more we truly love God, the more we'll love our neighbors and most particularly those bound to us by the sweet cords of natural love.

Another danger when we discover the beauty of an intense spiritual life is to yield to its delights while neglecting the obvious duties to which God calls us. In his admirable *Introduction to the Devout Life*, St. Francis de Sales emphatically asserts that no religious devotion is ever to disrupt family life. Just imagine a wife spending so much time reading holy books that the household is neglected, the children uncared for, and the husband treated as a piece of furniture (or worse: as a hopeless sinner because he doesn't share her religious ardor)! Dickens admirably caricatured this spiritual danger in the character of Mrs. Jellyby in *Bleak House,* who is so concerned with her social work for an obscure African tribe that she mercilessly neglects her family.

While I'm not a prophet, there's one thing I can guarantee: the more you live in the presence of God, relating everything you do to Him, hearkening to His voice, recognizing the theme He places in front of you, and dying to yourself — the more you do this, the more beautiful your relationship to Michael will become.

You'll learn to control all those things you've been concerned about recently — your sharp tongue, your critical sense, your humor which can be devastating when it's not tempered by sweet charity. Michael will quickly discover that your deepened spirituality is at the root of these felicitous changes. He won't object to religious practices which don' t bother him (because you do them discreetly) and which even obviously benefit him.

You probably have never heard of Elisabeth Leseur, a French woman who lost her faith after marrying a man who was an ardent atheist. They loved each other and had a good marriage, but eventually she realized that a marriage without God is crippled: something essential is lacking.

Elisabeth found her way back to God and began to lead an intense spiritual life. However, to avoid conflict with her atheistic husband, she was so discreet about it that her husband never realized she'd become an ardent Roman Catholic, having rediscovered on a deeper level the same faith that she had abandoned when she was only a youth.

Elisabeth died relatively young, and having kept a diary relating her spiritual transformation, she left a living testimony of the workings of grace in her soul. Her husband found this precious document after her death and only then discovered how deeply she had suffered from his atheism and from the fact that she couldn't share with him the deepest secrets of her soul. He was struck by grace, converted, and became a priest. (Later as a priest, he would shock the unaware in his congregation when he spoke of his "beloved wife.")

Michael doesn't seem, as yet, to share your longing for a more intense, God-centered life. So it's best that you follow Elisabeth Leseur's example by being loving, understanding, and generous. I'm sure that in God's good time you'll have the joy of sharing your spiritual life with Michael. What a beautiful prospect to look forward to!

With all my love and affection for both of you,

Lily

"Our baby's due in June!"

Dear Julie,

The great news finally came: you're expecting a child! I read and then re-read your letter several times — to assure myself that it was truly so. This news has been singing in my soul all day, so I've seized the very first opportunity to write to you.

The two great human mysteries in life are the love between husband and wife, and the fertility of this love. Love gives life! Who could imagine anything more beautiful than the fact that a child is conceived because his parents long for the most complete union that can exist between two human beings?

Now it is your inestimable privilege to have new life blossom in your womb: the mysterious fruit of your common love. Gratitude, reverence, awe, and love are the only proper responses to this event, which is why you're so overwhelmed. Your little baby, now so tiny, isn't just a conglomerate of cells; he's a human person, made in God's image and destined to enjoy His sight forever in Heaven.

How I wish that all women who have conceived would meditate upon this and thank God, who has allowed them to partake in the mystery of His creativity! Indeed, Chesterton is right when he writes that when you think about the mystery of giving birth, you start doubting the equality of the sexes. He calls child-bearing a "frightful female privilege."

I recall that when you fell in love with Michael you told me you started worrying about him: you trembled when he was traveling and didn't come home on time, when he was sick, when he was unhappy.

Now that you're carrying his child in your womb, you'll start trembling anew: is this little one healthy? Is everything developing normally? This loving fear will accompany you until you and your child are finally safe in heaven together, safe from the dangers of this world.

This may help you to understand why Michael is also overwhelmed by the news of your pregnancy and oscillates between pride and apprehension about this event which so profoundly alters your lives.

Now the mystery of your faithful love is crowned with the gift of new life growing in your womb: a child who will bring suffering but also great joy, and who will bring you closer to Michael than ever before.

From now on, you are *three,* no longer *two.* Michael fears both the changes that must take place and the new responsibilities he must shoulder. Help him to adjust by sharing with him your experiences during pregnancy; tell him your hopes for the little babe in your womb.

Let Michael know of your growing confidence in him so that as your pregnancy develops and you become more dependent on him, Michael can grow stronger as husband, father, and protector.

In the coming months, you and Michael should strive to awaken and nurture in each other a deep love for this little child and a profounder love for each other. I'm sure you have unparalleled happiness ahead of you.

When you're fearful, you both must remember that this child belongs primarily to God, and that God loves him infinitely more than you can. Kneel together and confide your child to God in your daily prayers and He'll take better care of the child than you can, because He's all-powerful.

My dear Julie, seeing you and Michael mature in your love for each other has been such a gift to me. What adventures you've had together!

From the bliss of your honeymoon to the problems that have afflicted you, you've persevered in love. In

Our baby's due in June!

good times and in bad, you've remembered that although marriage is a deed of daring, it's also the school of love. Together, you and Michael have triumphed over many difficulties because you've experienced the profound joy of faithful love. And you've learned the most important lesson any couple can learn: marriage is worth fighting for.

My heart is singing! I rejoice with you and for you!

Affectionately,

Lily

References

"By Love Refined" (Title)

"If any, so by love refin'd,/That he soul's language understood": John Donne, "The Ecstasy"

"And pregnant women, having their imaginations refined by love, even impress their hopes on the flesh of their infants": St. Francis de Sales, *Treatise on the Love of God*, Book VI, Ch. 15

"Love is a great thing!"

"Love is a great thing": Thomas à Kempis, *Imitation of Christ*, Book III, Ch. 5

"It is truly a deed of daring": Sören Kierkegaard, *Either/Or,* II

"Setting up house takes so much work!"

The German author Johann Wolf gang von Goethe used this stained-glass window analogy.

"Yes, he's the right man for me."

Gospel story of the Transfiguration: Mt. 17:2; Mk. 9:2

"I just can't be cheerful in the morning."

"It's easier to be a lover than a husband": Honoré de Balzac, *Physiologie du Mariage* (quoted in *A Book of French Quotations* compiled by Norbert Guterman).

"So many parties!"

"I-Thou": Cf. Dietrich von Hildebrand, *Metaphysik der Gemein-
schaft*, Ch. 2 and also *Humanae Vitae: A* Sign *of Contradiction*,
Pt . I, 6

"I wish it would bring us closer"

"Seek first the kingdom of God": Mt. 6:33

"It really hurt when he said that."

"Love believeth all things": 1 Cor 13:7

Credit of love: Dietrich von Hildebrand, *Das Wesen
der Liebe, III*

"We were so glad to see you."

"Reverence is *the* attitude which can be designated as the
mother of all moral life": Cf. Dietrich von Hildebrand, *Fundamental Moral Attitudes*, Ch. 1

"What a moving talk Michael and I had!"

"What is worthwhile is never easy": Plate, *Republic*, VI, 497

"We had a great time at the Christmas concert."

"For by reason of the stream of beauty entering in through his
eyes there comes a warmth, whereby his soul's plumage is
fostered, and with that warmth the roots of the wings are
melted...the stump of the wing swells and...the whole soul is
furnished with wings": Plato, *Phaedrus*, 251

"I'm actually happy serving him!"

"There is nothing so certain to lead to inequality as identity": G.K. Chesterton, "Woman and the Philosophers"

"A man should pride himself more upon serving well than upon commanding well": Plato, *Laws*, VI, 762

"I want a dishwasher; he wants a stereo."

"A duchess may ruin a duke": G.K. Chesterton, *What's Wrong With the World*, Pt. III, Ch. 4 ('The Romance of Thrift')

"No two persons perhaps are to be found": John Henry Cardinal Newman, *The Idea of the University*, Discourse 2

"I thought he'd like the plans I made for us."

"One mind, one soul, and one heart": An English translation of the title of Marcel Clément's very beautiful book on marriage: *Un Seul Cur, Line Seule Ame, Une Seule Chair,* Editions de L'Escalade, Paris, 1977

Fusion vs. union: Cf. Dietrich von Hildebrand, *Das Wesen der Liebe*, Ch. 6 and *Humanae Vitae: A Sign of Contradiction*, Pt. II, 4

"A lot of little things irritate me."

"Don't let the sun set on your wrath": Eph. 4:26

"Baseball bores me and Michael doesn't like art."

"God loves a cheerful giver": 2 Cor. 9:7

"My plans for the evening were ruined."

"Truly, I say unto you, unless you turn and become like children, you will never enter the kingdom of heaven": Mt. 18:3

"I'm still mad at him."

"It's not enough to be right": G. Marcel, *Le Quatuor en Fa Dièze*

"If only he had listened to me."

"Now is the time to get rid of self-will in him, punishing him, but not so as to disgrace him": Plato, *The Laws*, VII, 793

"Do you mean it's wrong to criticize Michael?"

"These also my heart hated, but not with a perfect hatred: for perchance I hated them more because I was to suffer by them, than because they did things utterly unlawful": St. Augustine, *Confessions*, Bk. V, 12

"I don't worry about dressing well."

"St. Paul [1 Tim. 2:9] desires that devout women, and the same may be said of men, should be attired 'in decent apparel, adorning themselves with modesty and sobriety'": St. Francis de Sales, *Introduction to the Devout Life*, Pt. III, Ch. 25

"Why shouldn't I just be myself?"

Valid/invalid feelings: Cf. Dietrich von Hildebrand, *Ethics*, Ch. 25

"It's so hard to change."

Transformation in Christ is published by Sophia Institute Press, Box 5284, Manchester, NH 03108.

"But what *every* individual loves most more than his only child, the child of promise, more than his only beloved on earth and in heaven is his own will": Sören Kierkegaard, *Christian Discourses*, Pt. 1, Ch. VII

"I'm putting in a lot of overtime."

"The only happiness is love, which is attained by giving, not receiving": Malcolm Muggeridge, *The Green Stick,* Ch. 1

"Our marriage just hasn't been the same lately."

"To what is said of eternal life, that there is no sighing and no tears, one can add: there is no habit": Sören Kierkegaard, *Works of Love*, Pt .1, Ch. II, A

"He's been hard to live with this week."

Marriage: The Mystery of Faithful Love is published by Sophia Institute Press, Box 5284, Manchester, NH 03108.

"Maybe I criticize him too much."

St. Monica's story: Cf. St. Augustine, *Confessions*, IX, 9

"I asked him to forgive me."

"Pride quits the human heart the moment love enters it": Théophile Gautier, *Mademoiselle de Maupin,* quoted in *A Book of French Quotations* compiled by Norbert Guterman

"He forgot our engagement anniversary!"

"In the image of God he created him: male and female he created them": Gen. 1:27

"I can't ignore all of his faults."

"Love believeth all things": 1 Cor. 13:7

"Love is patient and kind": 1 Cor 13:4-7

"Michael's colleague cares only about money."

"Abandon all hope of the ascent": Dante, *Divine Comedy, Hell*, Canto I, Line 54

"He alone can fulfill my immense desires": St. Thérèse of Lisieux, Manuscript A, Folio 81 (to Mother Agnes of Jesus); "Are not my immense desires a mere dream, a sort of madness?": Manuscript B, Folio 4 (to Sister Mary of the Sacred Heart)

"I thought I knew how to love."

"Immediately the father of the child cried out and said, 'I believe; help my unbelief!' ": Mk. 9:24

"I'm learning to forgive myself."

"The sacrifice acceptable to God is a broken spirit;/A broken and contrite heart, O God, Thou wilt not despise": Ps. 51:17

"I've been trying to pray more."

True devotion "not only does no injury to any vocation or employment; on the contrary it adorns and beautifies it": St. Francis de Sales, *Introduction to the Devout Life*, I, Ch. 3

"Our baby's due in June!"

"No one, staring at that frightful female privilege, can quite believe in the equality of the sexes": G.K. Chesterton, *What's Wrong With the World*, Pt. III, Ch. 10 ('The Higher Anarchy")

Alice von Hildebrand, Ph.D.

Seventeen-year-old Alice M. Jourdain came to America from her native Belgium in 1940. In 1944, she received her B.A. from Manhattanville College and in 1949 her Ph.D. in philosophy from Fordham University. At Fordham, she studied philosophy under the renowned European exile philosopher and anti-Nazi fighter, Dr. Dietrich von Hildebrand, whose thought she mastered and whose wife and best collaborator she later became.

In 1947, Alice von Hildebrand was hired as the first woman to teach philosophy at Hunter College (CUNY) in New York City, where she remained a faculty member for 37 years. At her retirement in 1984, she received the prestigious Presidential Award for Excellence in Teaching.

Alice von Hildebrand is at home in five languages and many countries. She has given hundreds of lectures throughout the United States, South America, and Europe, has appeared on dozens of radio and television talk

215

shows, and is a trustee of the Franciscan University of Steubenville.

In addition to *By Love Refined,* Alice von Hildebrand's published works include one book *(Introduction to a Philosophy of Religion)* and over 50 articles. With Dietrich von Hildebrand, she collaborated on a number of major works and with him co-authored *The Art of Living.*

Alice von Hildebrand currently has in preparation numerous other works, including books on wisdom, widowhood, feminism, C.S. Lewis, Kierkegaard, and Plato. She is also editing her late husband's *Memoirs.*

In recent years, Alice von Hildebrand has specialized in matters pertaining to women's issues, particularly love and marriage, as well as the role of religion in modern life. Her keen understanding of the human condition, her profound wisdom, and her great tenderness have won her the devotion of thousands of students spanning three generations.

Her hectic lecture and interview pace has picked up in recent years as more and more people discover Alice von Hildebrand – this remarkable Renaissance woman who embodies the deepest wisdom of our civilization.

Sophia Institute Press®

Sophia Institute is a nonprofit institution that seeks to restore man's knowledge of eternal truth, including man's knowledge of his own nature, his relation to other persons, and his relation to God.

Sophia Institute Press® serves this end in numerous ways: it publishes translations of foreign works to make them accessible for the first time to English-speaking readers; it brings out-of-print books back into print; and it publishes important new books that fulfill the ideals of Sophia Institute. These books afford readers a rich source of the enduring wisdom of mankind.

Sophia Institute Press® makes these high-quality books available to the general public by using advanced technology and by soliciting donations to subsidize its general publishing costs. Your generosity can help Sophia Institute Press® to provide the public with editions of works containing the enduring wisdom of the ages. Please send your tax-deductible contribution to the address below. We also welcome your questions, comments, and suggestions.

For your free catalog, call:
Toll-free: 1-800-888-9344

or write:
Sophia Institute Press®
Box 5284, Manchester, NH 03108

or visit our website:
www.sophiainstitute.com

Sophia Institute is a tax-exempt institution
as defined by the Internal Revenue Code,
Section 501(c)(3). Tax I.D. 22-2548708.